SECTION 1
CORPORATION BASICS

CORPORATION BASICS

WHAT IS A CORPORATION?

A corporation can be defined as "a separate and distinct entity that acts for, or on the behalf of a group of people". A corporation is in all respects, an artificial "person", created by the grace of state law, to act for, or on the behalf of, its owners.

Initially, the corporation was devised as a method of letting a group of owners act as one, much the same way a partnership would, with one important advantage. Since the corporation was a separate legal entity capable of being sued, it could take the blame if anything went wrong, thus protecting its owners. When the first corporations were formed years ago, the group of owners had to petition the state legislature to pass a special law creating this "privilege". Needless to say, incorporation was a business option available to only the rich and powerful, those with enough money and lawyers to have such a preferential law passed. This is how lawyers became involved with incorporations.

However, as time went by, state governments realized that the income taxes on corporations could create generous revenues. So, to increase the number of corporations, they began to create special sets of laws that would allow anyone to set up, and benefit from a corporation quickly and easily. In most states, the process has been reduced to the completing and filing of a simple, one page form. Unfortunately, many people are unaware that incorporating a business has been made this easy.

Once set up, this "artificial" entity has most of the rights and privilege that you have. In most cases, its abilities are identical to an individual's. A corporation can operate businesses, buy goods and services, sell goods and services, make contracts, rent office space, have checking and saving accounts, maintain retirement plans for its employees, sue, and be sued.

Although it is a legal "person", a corporation, can't walk, talk, think, or act for itself. It can't hold a pen to sign contracts. It can't go to the bank to make a deposit, nor can it plan a marketing strategy for its products.

Because of this, the business affairs of the corporation are managed and "directed" by what are known as directors, or "the board of directors". Directors are like the guardians of an incompetent adult who has rights, but can't act for himself. Directors meet from time to time to plan and approve what actions the corporation will take to conduct its business.

In large corporations, directors are not usually employees of the corporation. They are more like special consultants who come in periodically to plan and approve corporate actions. In return for their "direction", the directors usually receive a token compensation, and other perks.

In most large corporations, being a director is more a position of status, and in such a case, the directors merely meet periodically to "rubber stamp" what the officers have decided is best for the corporation. This "rubber stamp" approval of corporate action is not the correct procedure, but is the reality in larger corporations. Although directors are responsible for managing and directing the business affairs of the corporation, they mostly oversee the "big picture".

To manage the day to day activities of the corporation, the directors appoint and hire officers. Officers handle all of the day to day decisions that must be made to run a business, and the scope of their duties usually depends on the size of the corporation. That is, the president of a corporation like Sears probably delegates the important duty of selecting new store sites to a subordinate, but he would be directly involved in the acquisition of another large company like Dean Witter Reynolds for Sear's financial services division. In contrast, the president of a small business would probably do everything from selecting the store site to selling the merchandise. A corporation usually has the following officers:

A President ....Who carries out the most important functions.
A Vice-President ....Who can act for the President when needed.
A Secretary ....Who takes care of the corporate records and meetings.
A Treasurer ....Who manages the financial affairs of the corporation.

When managing the daily activities of the corporation, the president is generally responsible for the more important or glamorous responsibilities like signing contracts or creating strategies for the corporation. The vice-president fills in for the president when necessary, or assists the president. The secretary maintains corporate records and correlates the organizational affairs of the corporation. The treasurer is responsible for the financial welfare of the corporation, from obtaining loans, to overseeing the accounting department. This paragraph describes the duties of officers in a larger corporation. In smaller corporations however, most, or all of these positions may be filled by a single person who may carry out most, or all of these responsibilities.

Many times, in a small corporation, the directors and the officers are actually the same people who simply "wear different hats". That is, when one is carrying out director responsibilities, he's a director, and when he's taking care of officer responsibilities, he's an officer. Officers are most always employees of the corporation, and are eligible for all employee benefits, like retirement plans.

That explains who directs and manages the business, but the most important players in the average corporation aren't the directors or the officers. The most important people are those for whom the corporation was formed - the stockholders. The stockholders are the people who started, and own the corporation for their mutual benefit.

The stockholders invest money, property, or something else of value into the corporation, and in return for their investment, the stockholders will own a part of the corporation, relative to the amount they invested. These investments are the means by which the corporation is able buy machinery, inventories, rent buildings and start operations.

To provide evidence of their ownership of the corporation, the corporation will issue the shareholders a stock certificate. That's why these people are called stock"holders". These stocks, represent ownership in a particular corporation, and are bought and sold on the stock exchanges in New York. Of course, only larger corporation stocks are traded on an exchange. Although, in smaller corporations with more than two shareholders, stocks can trade between the shareholders or be bought by outsiders, just like they do on the large exchanges. In fact, the selling of stocks in a small corporation can actually be more competitive than events on Wall Street.

The stockholders control the corporation for their common good by appointing the directors who will oversee the activities of the corporation. In a large corporation, the directors are somewhat like referees that make sure the game is played fairly, and that no disagreements occur.

Since the directors, who meet irregularly, aren't there all the time, they hire officers to run the business on a daily basis. Of course this is the textbook example of a large corporation, and is some what different than a small one, but is explained so that you may gain a fuller understanding of all the participants in the corporate world. You may understand the process better by reviewing this diagram:

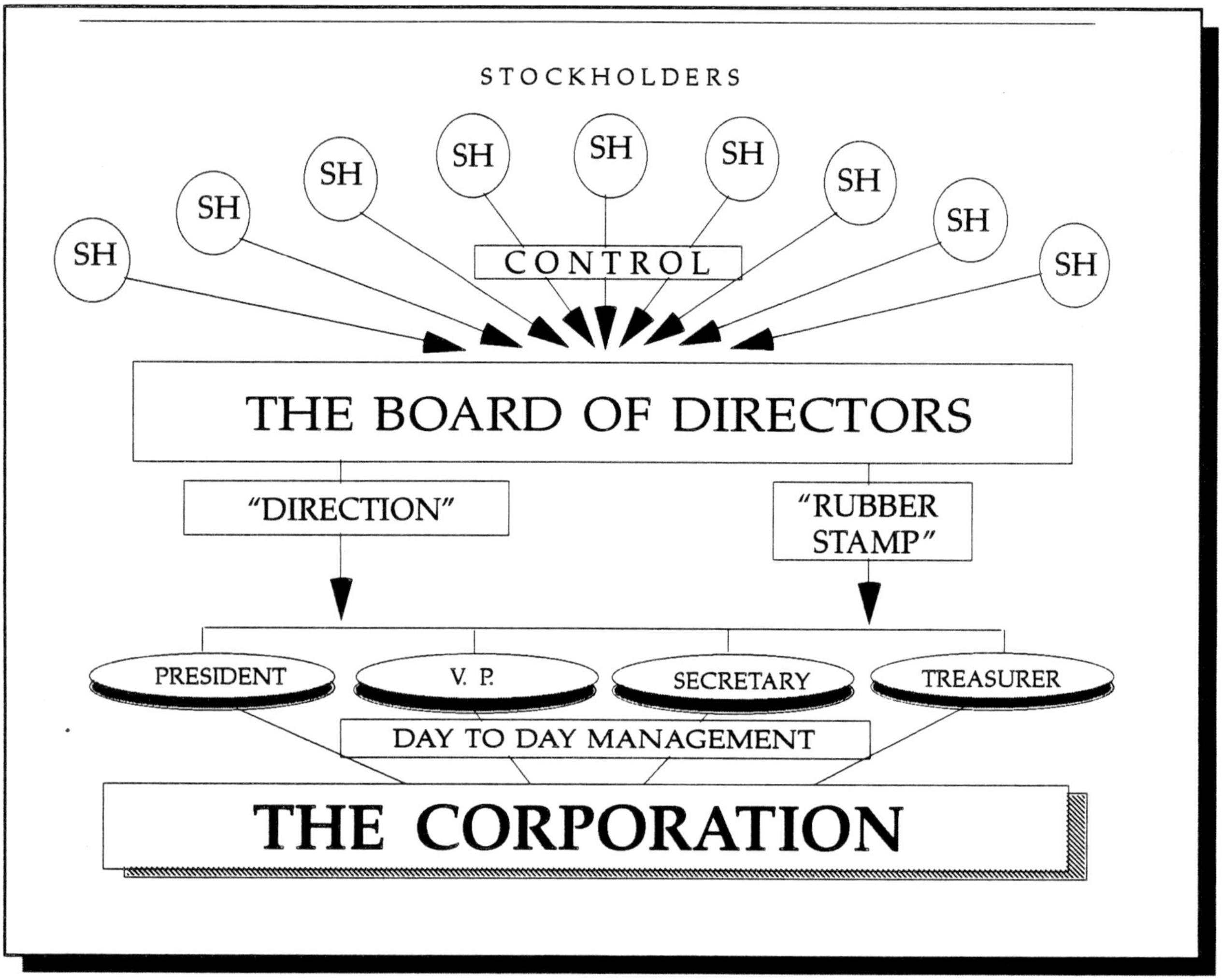

Unlike this diagram, the next figure will show you that the typical small corporation, like you are forming, is somewhat different from the textbook example of a large corporation. The main difference, as you have probably already determined, is the number of people involved. In a small corporation, the business owner is usually the only stockholder, the only director, and the only officer.** In this instance, the corporation would look more like the next example:

** *Depending on which state you are in.*

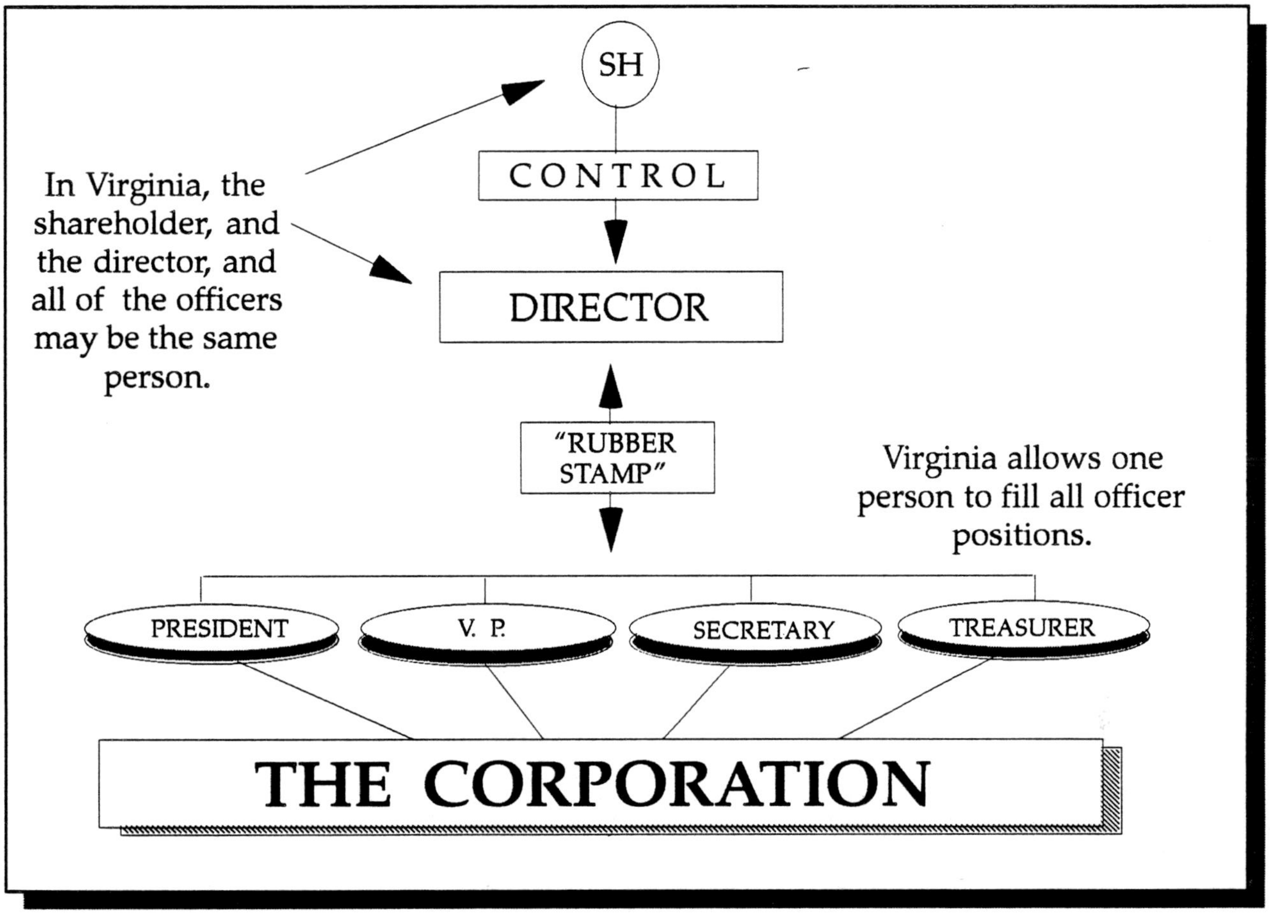

This is the typical example of a small corporation. Virginia allows a corporation to be formed with only one person, who could fill all the positions shown above. However, many businesses are formed with more than two people, in which case the persons involved can hold one or more positions. The various combinations of these positions is up to the shareholders.

WHAT WILL INCORPORATING DO FOR YOU?

To answer this question, you must understand some basic principles about how businesses are structured. The most common small business structures are the "sole proprietorship" and the "partnership". Other than some bookkeeping differences, these two forms of organizing a business are basically the same, with the exception of the number of people involved. The sole proprietorship is, as the name suggests, one person. The partnership is comprised of two or more people.

The sole proprietorship and the partnership differ from the corporation because the sole proprietorship and the partnership are inseparable from the owner of the business. Remember that the corporation is a separate and distinct entity from its owners, created to "take the heat" for them. However, in the case of the sole proprietorship and the partnership, the owner IS the business, and business IS the owner. This inseparability creates personal liability and tax problems.

For example, if Bob Jones owns an **unincorporated** business called Jones Advertising, the legal name of the business is actually "Bob Jones, doing business as (dba) Jones Advertising". The name "Jones Advertising" is an alias for Bob Jones himself. If something happens to Bob, this Jones Advertising would actually cease to exist.

If Bob has the foresight to leave the business **assets**** to his wife Mary, Jones Advertising could be reborn as a new company operated by his wife. This time, the company would be known as Mary Jones, dba Jones Advertising, legally, and technically a new company. Mary will have to open a new bank account and obtain a new tax identification number from the Internal Revenue Service for the "new" business.

The sole proprietorship and the partnership function like this example.

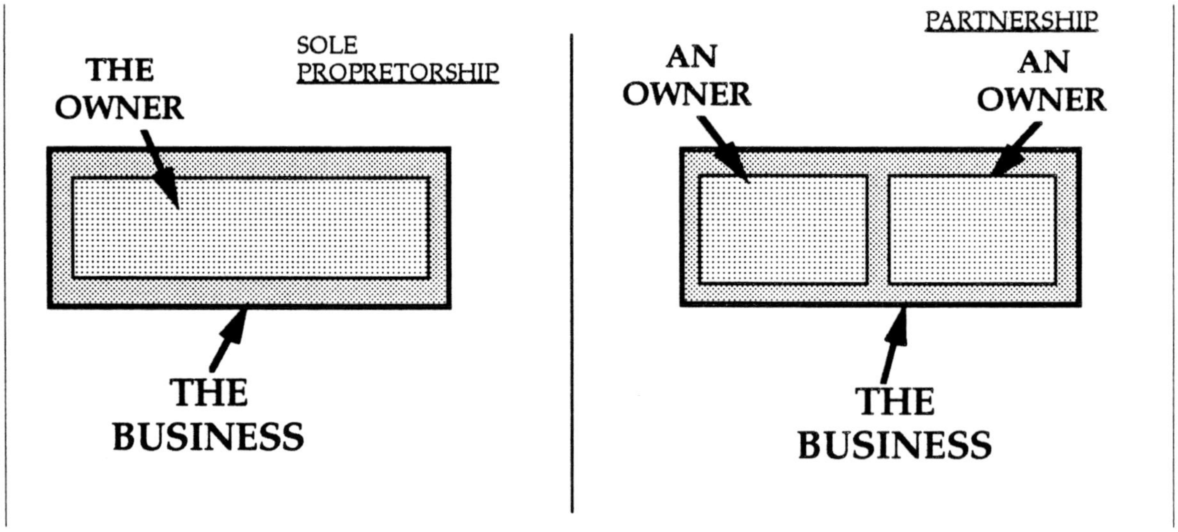

As you can see, the business and the person(s) owning the business are the same. In contrast, the figure describing corporations shows that the corporation is separate and distinct from all those who own and control it. This separation of the owners and managers from the business is very advantageous. When a business is not incorporated, the inseparability of the business and the owner is the cause of two major problems:

** *He couldn't leave the business, as it has ceased to exist. He could only leave her the assets of the business.*

Problem 1:

Since you (the business owner) ***are*** *the business, whoever sues the business sues you.*

Problem 2:

According to the IRS, health insurance, pension plans, and other "employee" benefit plans are for employees only. Since you ***are*** *the business (and the employer), you may not participate in "employee" benefit plans. Your benefits are not tax deductible expenses. (You have to pay for* ***your*** *insurance out of your pocket, while paying for your employees' benefits with pretax dollars.)*

Incorporating basically solves both of these problems. Separating the owner (the shareholder) from the business protects him. Since the corporation has the right to sue and be sued, the person bringing a suit will typically sue the corporation. So, the stockholder is not sued, the corporation is. This is the case even if the owner is the only shareholder, the only director, and one of the officers. For example, if someone sues Ford Motor Company, the person bringing the suit will simply sue the corporation, and Mr. Ford will hardly be involved at all.

As far as employee benefits are concerned, incorporating allows you to participate as an employee and let the corporation "pick up the tab" for your benefits. You see, when your business is incorporated, the corporation, **a separate entity**, is the employer - **not** you. You just happen to be the owner of the corporation that you work for, an advantageous position to be in.

Then how do you become an employee? Most people "hire" themselves as officers or other employees of the corporation. Remember, officers are usually employees of the corporation, and as an employee, you can now participate in employee benefit programs. This kit was constructed so that the officers are the initial employees of the corporation, making them eligible for employee benefits.

TAX SAVING STRATEGIES

As discussed above, operating your business as a corporation offers you substantial advantages. The tax breaks you will enjoy personally, and the tax dollars you'll save are some of the best. In this section we will briefly discuss some of the most profitable tax saving strategies that are available. You will need to discuss these strategies with your tax professional, or insurance specialist. Sometimes, a **good,** tax planning, insurance person knows as much about these advanced strategies as the average tax professional. No matter what, investigate these options. If your tax planner doesn't know about these strategies, or how they work, look until you find one who does. Another excellent reference that you may use is a book on the subject called "USE YOUR OWN CORPORATION TO GET RICH", by Judith H. McQuown.

The best tax saving strategies are those that allow you to personally benefit from fringe benefits that your corporation pays for. Why? Because this way you gain very lucrative perks that you are not taxed on personally. For providing you with these perks, your corporation gets a tax deduction, lowering it's tax bill. While larger corporations offer these perks to attract and keep good employees, the owners of small corporations do it to obtain IRS approved tax-free benefits. Although there are a dozen strategies that utilize this principal, we have outlined the four most beneficial here: They are:

- A Pension Plan
- Medical Insurance
- A Medical reimbursement Plan
- A "Free" Life Insurance Plan

• A Pension Plan

Most everyone is familiar with pension plans. They are the company sponsored retirement accounts that most larger companies, and more and more smaller companies offer to their employees. Pension plans basically come in two types, either "defined benefit" plans, or "defined contribution" plans. A defined benefit plan is a plan that allows you to contribute different amounts each year, but pays you a set, or "defined" amount at retirement. On the other hand, a defined contribution plan is one that requires the same fixed contribution each year, but payout upon retirement is based on a flexible schedule.

The best thing about a pension plan is that the contributions made into your account by your corporation are tax deductions for the corporation, but are not taxable to you until you retire. These contributions earn interest and multiply with no tax implications to you, while the corporation's tax bill is lowered by thousands of dollars per year. If you have an S corporation, making these contributions lowers your personal tax bill while putting large amounts away for your retirement. It's kind of like an IRA without the small annual limit.

If you have a C corporation, things can be even more lucrative. You can actually borrow money from the corporate pension plan if certain, easy to meet, requirements are met. Why would you want to borrow your own money? Well, first of all, it's not actually your money - not yet. It is money held in trust by your corporation for your retirement. It's not actually yours until the company writes you a check, at which point you'll have to give the IRS about a third for income taxes. But until then, you can still use the money, but without paying taxes on it! That's the best thing about borrowing from your own pension fund - the ability to use the money now, without incurring a tax liability. Since this money is being loaned to you, it is not income, and not taxable.

Of course, as with any loan, you'll have to pay interest, otherwise, it would not be considered a loan by the IRS, making it a taxable event for you. But you say, what's the use if I have to pay interest? Because, interest is cheaper that income taxes, and while income taxes are paid to the government, the interest you'll pay is paid to your pension fund, making the amount available at retirement even larger. Money paid in taxes you'll never see again, but money paid in interest on a pension fund loan is paid to your pension fund, increasing the size of your nest egg.

So, the bottom line is that you should borrow from your pension fund as often as you can, because you'll get to use funds without paying taxes on them, and the interest you'll pay only makes your pension fund larger. The only problem is that you can't borrow from your pension fund anytime you please. You can only borrow to:

1) Acquire, construct, or reconstruct your personal residence
2) **Pay college tuition**, or
3) To pay for medical treatment requiring "immediate, heavy financial need".

Also, loans must be made available to all participants in the pension plan. Of course, with a small business, the participants are usually all family anyway.

As with any loan, you'll have to get permission to borrow the money from the organization in charge of it. In this case, you'll have to get approval from the corporation, since the corporation is actually a separate entity. However, getting the approval is an easy thing to do when you own the corporation. Formal approval can be granted by taking a copy of one of the blank corporate consents, found in section five, on page number three, and typing this verbiage on the form.

"It has been decided by the board of directors of ____(corporation name)____ to entitle employees of the corporation, specifically ____(your name)_____ to borrow funds from the corporate pension plan. The proceeds of this loan will be used in accordance with Internal Revenue Code § 72. Terms and conditions for borrowing will be similar to those at local lending institutions and the interest rate may not exceed that allowed by state law. A promissory note will be executed and filed with the corporation, and be made a part of the public record located at the local county courthouse."

All directors must sign and date this consent showing their affirmative vote on the matter. Also, whoever is managing your pension fund, a stockbroker, bank trust department, etc., will need a copy of this consent. Finally remember to consult your CPA about this, as he will be up to date on the IRS codes and has probably done it before.

• Medical Insurance

One of the best things about having a corporation is letting the corporation pay the premiums for your medical, and dental insurance. Again, these benefits are generally not taxable to you, and don't come out of your paycheck. Letting the corporation pay for your medical insurance provides you with expensive benefits, while providing a tax deduction for the corporation.

• A Medical reimbursement Plan

A medical reimbursement plan is an employee benefit plan that allows the corporation to reimburse you for expenses incurred for things like insurance deductibles, insurance co-payments, eyeglasses, braces, etc.. You are probably beginning to see how beneficial a plan like this could be. Each year, we spend thousands of dollars on these items that even the best insurance doesn't pay for. Fortunately, with a corporation, we can let the corporation pick up the tab for these expensive items. A medical reimbursement plan like this can save the shareholder thousands of dollars per year, and provide the corporation a tax deduction. A medical reimbursement plan is a standard fill in the blank type form that can be found in most office supply stores, in the book by Judith H. McQuown described at the front of this section, or from your CPA. You will also need to type up a blank consent like the one outlined above that states that "the directors approve of and adopt the medical reimbursement plan".

• A "Free" Life Insurance Plan

The IRS allows a corporation to pay premiums for life insurance for its employees up to $50,000 in death benefits for each employee. Since the premiums for term life insurance for a younger person are low, this may not seem like much of a benefit, but to older business people, the amount can be substantial. This insurance plan can be quite profitable, and no matter what, it's "free", so take advantage of it. All you'll need to do, like you'll need to do every time the corporation does something important, is to draft a consent that says the directors approve of taking the action, and have all the directors sign it.

COMMONLY ASKED INCORPORATION QUESTIONS

In this section, we have compiled a list of many of the most commonly asked questions people have about incorporating. You should go through the entire list now, or at least skim the list to find questions similar to yours.

WHAT ARE THE ARTICLES OF INCORPORATION?
The ARTICLES OF INCORPORATION, sometimes called the CHARTER, declares the desire of an individual or group of individuals to become a corporation. It spells out certain minimum information about the corporation that is required by the laws of the state. It may also contain specific information about the corporation that needs to be made public record, like limited director liability and restricting the transfer of corporate stock.

WHAT IS AN ASSUMED NAME?
An assumed name, sometimes called a fictitious name, is a feature of some state corporation laws that allow a corporation to operate under more than one name. This can be quite convenient to the small business person who sells different products but does not wish to have several corporations. Many people initially name the corporation their last name like Jones, Inc., and then name their different companies to be more descriptive of the separate product lines, like Quantum Computers, Inc., and Standard Computer Software Corporation. All of these names are just different names, or aliases for the same corporation, that has only one set of books, and the same shareholders.

WHAT ARE AUTHORIZED SHARES?
State law specifies that shares of stock in the corporation will be issued under the direction of the board of directors. But, since the corporation is set up to benefit the shareholders, the shareholders set, or limit, the number of shares the directors are "authorized", or allowed, to issue. Since the directors are not allowed to issue shares without authorization from the shareholders, the number of authorized shares is equal to the number of total shares.

WHAT IS THE DIFFERENCE BETWEEN ISSUED AND AUTHORIZED SHARES ?
A corporation's charter, or the shareholders will "authorize" a certain number of shares of stock to be created for the corporation's present or future use. These shares are without value and in a sense, lie dormant unless they are "issued" to a shareholder. When stock is issued to someone, it represents a ownership in the corporation similar to the way a certificate of deposit represents ownership of funds deposited in a bank.

WHAT IS THE BOARD OF DIRECTORS?

The board of directors is the body of people specified by state law to direct and oversee the business affairs of the corporation. They meet infrequently, and usually hire officers to manage the day to day business operations.

WHAT ARE BYLAWS?

Just as a city or state government has laws for its citizens, the corporation has rules for its shareholders, officers, and directors. These rules are called the bylaws. They specify things like the number of votes required to pass a matter put before the corporation, and the requirements to be met before a shareholder can sell their stock.

WHAT IS A "C" CORPORATION?

The IRS, **not** the state, classifies corporations according to how they want to be taxed. There are two types of corporations according to the IRS, either "C" corporations, named after subchapter C of the tax code, or "S" corporations, named after subchapter S of the tax code. C corporations, since corporations are a separate and distinct entity, have their own tax identification number and pay their own taxes. S corporations on the other hand, sometimes called small business corporations, are taxed as if the business was a partnership. Similar to a partnership, an S corporation "passes through" its income or losses to the shareholder's personal tax returns and is not liable for Federal income taxes itself. The shareholders of an S corporation will pay personal income taxes based on the income of the S corporation, whether or not the shareholder received any of the income. Conversely, the S corporation shareholders will be able to personally enjoy any losses the corporation may have. You will need to discuss this matter with your CPA.

WHAT DOES CAPITALIZATION MEAN?

Capitalization is simply the amount of money that a corporation has in its "kitty" when operation begin. Some states have minimum capitalization requirements to provide a bare minimum of assets. Since shareholders are somewhat insulated from lawsuits against a corporation, these assets provide a means to pay any potential lawsuit winners. Minimum capitalization requirements also make it a little more difficult to start a corporation, thus helping to keep out the "riff raff".

WHAT IS A CERTIFICATE OF INCORPORATION?

The certificate of incorporation is what some states issue to evidence that yours is a valid corporation, and has satisfied the requirements for incorporating in the state.

WHAT IS A CHARTER?

The terms charter and articles of incorporation are used interchangeably. Please see WHAT ARE THE ARTICLES OF INCORPORATION?

WHAT ARE DIRECTORS?

Directors are the people who oversee the affairs of the corporation according to what they think is best for the corporation. Directors however, are like politicians, hand picked by the shareholders, and subject to being removed by the shareholders. In a small corporation the directors are usually the shareholders who simply put on their director's "hat" when the time calls.

WHAT IS A DIVIDEND?

A dividend is a special payment, or payments made on a quarterly basis, in either cash or additional stock, to the holders of shares in the corporation. This is in return for their initial investment in the corporation. It is much the same as interest on a loan except that the dividend is based on the income of the corporation, and may or may not be a regular payment. Dividends are also not deductible by the corporation while interest payments are.

WHAT IS AN INCORPORATOR?

The incorporator is simply the person that files the paperwork required by law to incorporate a business. The incorporator's duties and title end after incorporating.

WHAT ARE ISSUED SHARES?

Issued shares are easily confused with authorized shares. Authorized shares are the number of shares set by the ARTICLES that the board of directors is "authorized" to issue. Issued shares, however, is the number of shares "issued", or given out to shareholders. Only issued shares are counted for ownership purposes.

HOW MANY SHARES OF STOCK ARE REQUIRED?

A corporation can't be a corporation without at least one share of stock. So at a minimum you must have at least one shareholder, and one share of stock.

WHAT IS PAR VALUE?

Par value is simply an accounting or bookkeeping unit of measure used to keep track of the amounts given to the corporation in exchange for the issuance of stock. Par value means basically the same as purchase price. If the stock has a $1000 par value, then the person wishing to purchase the stock must give something with at least a $1000 value for the stock. Amounts given for the stock in excess of par value are called "paid in capital in excess of par value" and again is simply a bookkeeping title. Par value is only meaningful when the stock is bought directly from the corporation and is not considered when stock is bought on an exchange or on the open market. When one buys stock on an exchange, he pays the "market" price, the price that the market determines the stock is worth.

WHAT IS NO PAR VALUE STOCK?

Since par value more or less means the price to be paid for the shares when purchased from the corporation, no par value stock is stock for which no fixed price is set. This is usually the case in small corporations where the owners issue themselves a number of shares and simply infuse money in the corporation when needed.

MUST STOCK HAVE A PAR VALUE?

No. Most often in a small business corporation the stock is called "no par value stock" which simply means that there is no set amount of payment required to purchase the stock of the corporation. All amounts paid to the corporation for the stock of the corporation is called "paid in capital".

WHAT ARE OFFICERS?

The officers are responsible for duties outlined by the corporate bylaws. The officers are usually employees of the corporation and manage the business on a daily basis. In a small corporation, the officers are usually the directors, and the shareholders who merely "wear different hats". It may seem silly to have all this role playing, but a small corporation is set up according to the requirements of state laws which were made with large corporations in mind.

WHAT IS A REGISTERED AGENT?

The registered agent is the person to whom all legal correspondence will be sent. The reason a registered agent is needed is to make sure that the corporation will have an assigned representative at a known address to receive all legal documents on behalf of the corporation. Although a corporation is a separate legal entity, it cannot physically receive documents, and therefore needs a real person to receive them.

WHAT IS AN ANNUAL MEETING?

The annual meeting is a special meeting that legally **has to be held** once a year to "review the results of corporate operations" with the shareholders. Remember that corporation laws were written with large corporations in mind, where the shareholders do not participate in the business. With a small corporation, it is play acting. A standard MINUTES OF THE ANNUAL SHAREHOLDER MEETING sheet is included with this kit to satisfy the legal requirements simply and without play acting.

WHAT ARE STOCKHOLDERS?

The term stockholders and shareholders are usually used interchangeably. The shareholders are the people for whom the corporation was organized. With large corporations, shareholders are merely investors who put money into the business in return for future dividends. In a small corporation, the shareholders are the people who actually start and run the corporation.

VIRGINIA QUESTIONS

WHAT'S THE FEWEST NUMBER OF PEOPLE NEEDED TO INCORPORATE ?

One. You should have all the officers described previously, but all of these positions may be held by the same person. You should also have at least one director, named in the Articles. Finally, you should have at least one shareholder, but as said before, all of these positions can be held by one person.

HOW MANY DIRECTORS DOES THE CORPORATION NEED?

At least one. The director(s) manage the business affairs for the corporation, and enjoy some immunity from certain liabilities. All important business decisions should be made, and recorded as made, by the director(s).

HOW MANY OFFICERS DOES THE CORPORATION NEED?

You should have all four officer positions filled, but since all of these can be filled by one person, you will only need one person to fill all four positions.

IS THERE A CERTAIN AMOUNT OF CAPITAL REQUIRED TO INCORPORATE?

No. Some states require that you put a certain amount of money or property into the corporation before you can incorporate, but Virginia does not. In this case, the stock would be called "no par value stock". The IRS calls this a "thin Corporation", referring to the thin capitalization of the corporation.

WHAT IS A CORPORATE SEAL FOR?

The corporate seal is the way in which a corporation "signs" contracts and other official documents, like stock certificates. You should have a seal for these purposes. A seal may be obtained from most office supply stores. One of the best and least expensive we've ever seen is from GOES, the company we purchase our book covers and and stock certificates from. An order form is included in the back for your convenience. Also, purchasers of this book will get a 10% discount, and pay no sales tax. (TN pays tax.)

WHAT IS CONSIDERED VALID CONSIDERATION FOR STOCK?

You must buy stock from the corporation with payments approved by State law. You should pay money, give property, or have already provided labor or services to the corporation for which you were not paid. Of course, since you are on the Board of Directors, you" set the price" for the stock. So, as long as you pay some amount of money for the stock, you'll satisfy state requirements.

SECTION 2
THE INCORPORATING PROCESS

THE INCORPORATING PROCESS

Please read all of the steps and understand them fully before completing any step. A mistake could result in having to redo and refile paperwork, costing time and money.

The Corporation Commission of Virginia is the department of State government that is in charge of corporations. You will work with them now, and in the future when you need to make changes, or do something that requires the retrieving of recorded documents. Everyone we've spoken to at the Corporation Commission's office is very helpful and friendly. They can answer most any question that you might have about forming a corporation.

You may either mail, or hand deliver your documents to their office. Taking them yourself is convenient if you need to incorporate in a hurry, or simply prefer to speak to someone in person. If you want to mail your documents, you should mail them to the main office. The address and telephone number is as follows:

MAIN OFFICE
State Corporation Commission
1220 Bank Street
PO Box 1197
Richmond, VA 23219

Walk in, or telephone, (804) 786-3733

The incorporation process is very simple, and consists of five steps in two groups:

PART ONE Steps done with the State or County	**PART TWO** Steps done with shareholders, directors, and officers.
Step 2. Step 3.	Step 1. Step 4. Step 5.

The steps are summarized as follows:

Step 1. **CHOOSE A CORPORATE NAME**
Step 2. **CHECK THE AVAILABILITY OF "YOUR" NAME**
Step 3. **FILE YOUR PAPERWORK**
Step 4. **ORGANIZATIONAL MATTERS**
Step 5. **ISSUE THE STOCK OF THE CORPORATION**

STEP 1.
CHOOSE A CORPORATE NAME

The first step in organizing your corporation is selecting a name. The corporate name must meet specific requirements outlined by State law, and the Corporation Commission of Virginia. Your corporate name must meet the following two requirements:

> **A.** It must be distinguishable from other **corporate** names currently reserved, or used in Virginia, or other names registered with the Corporation Commission.
> **B.** It must include a specific word, or abbreviation of a word, that identifies the business as a corporation.

If you are a member of a licensed profession such as a CPA, Dentist, Architect, Engineer, etc., your name will need to meet professional regulatory requirements. You should check with your State licensing board to see what those requirements are.

The first requirement (**A.**) is almost self-explanatory. Simply, your name may not be the same as another corporate name already being used in Virginia. The name must be different because it would be confusing to the public, and possibly damaging to the company who held initial claim to the name, if names could be repeated. For example, if there were ten companies in the state calling themselves Federal Express Corp., we wouldn't know who the real Federal Express overnight package carrier was. In addition, allowing more than one company to use the same name would lead to confusion when someone wanted to file suit against a corporation.

Step number two will discuss how to see if the name you like is already being used. For now, you need to decide exactly what your corporate name will be, and consider a couple of alternatives in case your first choice is unavailable. The telephone book is an excellent place to shop for a name, remembering of course that your name must be distinguishable from the names you find there.

When choosing your name, care must be taken if the name you prefer is a common one. Because if it is, someone is probably already using it. For example, if you wanted to name your corporation Brown, Inc., you're more than likely out of luck. The name Brown is so common, its use was probably taken by another corporation long ago.

However, if your name is Brown and you wanted to use it in your business, there is still a way to do it. All you have to do is change the name slightly, just enough to distinguish it from others. For example, instead of using Brown, Inc., you could add your first name or initial, and name your corporation William Brown, Inc., or D. Brown, Incorporated. You can add a descriptive word or two, and name the corporation like these examples:

Brown **Ventures**, Inc.	Brown **Construction** , Inc.
Brown **Brothers**, Inc.	**Virginia** Brown, Inc.
Brown **Enterprises**, Inc.	Brown **& Company**, Inc

Although all these examples contain Brown, Inc., they are dissimilar enough to satisfy the requirements of most states.

The second requirement a corporate name must satisfy (**B**.), is an easy one to meet. All you have to do is include as a part of your name, one of the following words. We will refer to them as "Inc." words.

Incorporated, or its abbreviation, **Inc**.
Corporation, or its abbreviation, **Corp**.

These "Inc." words distinguish the business as a corporation. Below are some of the possible uses of these terms. You can tell by the names of these businesses that they all are incorporated:

Brown **Incorporated**	Brown, **Inc.**
The Brown **Corporation**	The Brown **Corp.**
Brown & Company, **Inc.**	The Brown **Corporation, Inc.**

STEP 2.
CHECK THE AVAILABILITY OF "YOUR" NAME

Now that you've chosen the name you wish to use, you'll need to see if another corporation in the state is already using it. To do this, call the office of the Corporation Commission. Their telephone number is **(804) 786-3733**. Checking the availability of "your" name should only take a couple of minutes, and this is also a good time to ask the Corporation Commission any questions that you may have. Generally, afternoons are a better time to call, because the volume of transactions is slightly lower.

Before you call the Corporation Commission, be sure of the name you wish to use, and that it contains one of the required "Inc." words. Also, you should have one or two additional names chosen, in case your first choice is being used by another corporation.

The Corporation Commission has immediate access to all corporate names being used by corporations in the state by computer. The role playing outlined below is designed for a telephone call, but of course face to face conversation will be the same. The conversation will basically go like this:

SEC./STATE: Corporation Commission, may I help you?

YOU: Yes. I'd like to check the availability of a corporate name please. (The person will either check the name, or transfer you to the person who will.)

SEC./STATE: Okay. What is the name you'd like to check?

YOU: Brown Advertising, Inc.
(The person will now check their computer for the name.)

SEC./STATE: That name appears to be available. (That's what you want to hear.)

YOU: Thank You.

The Corporation Commission will usually only say something to the effect that the "name **appears** to be available". That's because someone may walk into their office five minutes later and file paperwork using "your" name. **There are no guarantees as to the availability of names until your paperwork is accepted.** The name will not be officially yours until either an application to reserve the name, or ARTICLES OF INCORPORATION is accepted and filed by the Corporation Commission.

If you're first choice for a corporate name is already being used, the conversation will usually continue like this:

SEC./STATE: Brown Advertising does not appear to be available at this time. Are there any other names you'd like to check? (This is when your second and third choices come in handy.)

YOU: Yes. What about Brown Brothers Advertising, Inc.?

SEC./STATE: (The person will now check their computer for the new name) That name does appear to be available at this time. (You've hit pay dirt.)

YOU: Thank You.

Now that you've learned at least one of your names is available, you have **two** choices:

FIRST CHOICE - Reserve the name for your future use, or

SECOND CHOICE - File your ARTICLES OF INCORPORATION.

The first choice should be made if you are not ready to file your incorporation paperwork. To reserve the name, you must file a special application that reserves the name for your exclusive use for a **120** day period. It's called APPLICATION FOR RESERVATION OF CORPORATE NAME (included in this section). If you are not ready to incorporate and are concerned about losing "your" name, your only choice is to file the application to reserve the name. Currently, the fee charged by the Corporation Commission to file this application is **$10.00.**

Your second choice is to go ahead and file your incorporation paperwork, a form known as the ARTICLES OF INCORPORATION, included in this section. Since there is the additional fee charged to reserve the name, most people simply "lock up" their name by filing the ARTICLES OF INCORPORATION. Either way, you should waste no time in filing one of these documents. If you delay, you could lose "your" name to someone else.

STEP 3.
FILE YOUR PAPERWORK

The paperwork you must file to incorporate a business in Virginia consists of a one page form, included with this kit, called the ARTICLES OF INCORPORATION. The ARTICLES OF INCORPORATION are very simple to complete if you know a few basic facts like your name, the corporation's name, and your address. You should type the form, because typing helps insure its correct recording, and reduces the chance of your Articles being returned because of poor penmanship. Line by line instructions are as follows:

Article 1: Insert your corporate name in the space provided.

Article 2: If you have an office address, put it in the space provided. It must be a street address with the ZIP code or the ARTICLES OF INCORPORATION may be refused. If your home is your office, put that address here. Also, in the space provided, put the name of the county in which this address is located

Article 3: The registered agent is the person to whom all legal correspondence will be sent. The incorporator is simply the person who files the paperwork to form the corporation. You will put your name in the space provided.

Article 4: Nothing is required for you to do here. Many corporations issue 1,000 shares of stock. This is a good round number that allows for some stock to be issued to stockholders now, while leaving some stock to be issued to new stockholders later. Pre-emptive rights pertain to the offering of **new** shares to existing shareholders before they are offered to outsiders. Preemptive rights try to prevent the "squeezing out" of a smaller shareholder by those with enough money to buy the newly issued stock, thereby increasing their voting power at the expense of the little guy. Article 4 is stated in a way to protect all shareholders equally.

Article 5: In the space provided, specify exactly what the corporation will do to make a profit. A few examples might be, "to publish books", "to sell computers", or "to develop real estate".

Article 6: Nothing is required for you to do here.

Article 7: Put the number of directors in the space provided, and below that, their names and business addresses, or other street address.

After completing the ARTICLES and double checking them for accuracy, you will need to sign and date them with <u>black</u> ink. All those involved in the corporation do **<u>not</u>** need to sign the ARTICLES because the ARTICLES will be formally adopted by all shareholders and directors **after** the ARTICLES return from the Corporation Commission's Office. So, only the person completing the ARTICLES (the incorporator) needs to sign.

Now you are ready to file your ARTICLES. You will send the Corporation Commission the original ARTICLES, the Charter fee of fifty dollars ($50), and the filing fee of twenty-five ($25) dollars. You may want to verify the amount of the filing fee and incorporation tax when you call to check the availability of your corporate name.

The Charter fee is based on the number of shares of stock that you have. As this kit is set up, you will have 1000 shares of common, no par value stock. The Charter fee is fifty dollars for each 25,000 shares or less. So, with 1000 shares, your fee will be fifty dollars.

Finally, send the following items to the address below:

1. The original ARTICLES,
2. A check for $75.00, made payable to the Corporation Commission of Virginia. (This includes $50 for the Charter fee, and $25 for the filing fee.)

State Corporation Commission
1220 Bank Street
PO Box 1197
Richmond, VA 23219

When the documents are processed, the Corporation Commission will time and date stamp the Articles. The Articles will not be returned to you, instead, you will be sent official notification of your incorporation. You will retain this official notification with your corporate records.

If you reserved your name prior to filing the ARTICLES, you should bring this to the Corporation Commission's attention when you file the ARTICLES. You should do this in order to eliminate any confusion as to who has the right to use the name. To do this, simply write a note, or include a cover letter stating that you reserved the name for the corporation. You should include any official notification of your name reservation, keeping a copy for yourself.

STEP 4:
ORGANIZATIONAL MATTERS

State law requires that after ARTICLES OF INCORPORATION are filed, the ARTICLES and the bylaws must be adopted by the corporation, and the officers of the corporation appointed. This sounds complicated, but the whole process has been simplified for you. Included with this kit is a pre-written consent that does all of this. When you get your ARTICLES OF INCORPORATION back from the Corporation Commission, you'll need to complete, sign, and date the DIRECTORS CONSENT FOR ORGANIZATIONAL MATTERS in this section. This consent is properly worded to accomplish the tasks outlined above, and satisfy State law. All you'll need to do is fill in the blanks of the form with the appropriate names, and sign at the bottom. If you haven't decided what the officer salaries will be, leave these spaces blank until you know, but don't wait very long to complete the form.

STEP 5.
ISSUE THE STOCK OF THE CORPORATION

This is the final step in forming your corporation. Stock is issued to evidence a person's ownership in the corporation. All you'll need to do to issue the stock is complete, sign, and date the CONSENT TO ISSUE STOCK OF THE CORPORATION - and you'll be finished. This consent uses standard wording to satisfy State requirements. Please note that the words stock and shares both basically mean the same thing, and are usually used interchangeably.

First, the difference between authorized and issued shares of stock must be made clear. Authorized shares is the number of shares set by the ARTICLES that the board of directors is "authorized" to issue. The board of directors is the body that controls the issuance of stock. The board may issue all the shares now, or issue some now, and some later. Your ARTICLES, as this kit is set up, authorizes the board to issue 1000 shares of stock. In this case, the number of authorized shares equals the total number of shares. Issued shares, however, is the number of shares issued, or given out to shareholders. Only issued shares count for ownership purposes.

Shares that are not issued are called authorized but unissued shares. They are technically worthless until they are issued to a shareholder. Usually when a corporation issues shares of stock to its initial shareholders, a few shares are left unissued so that they may be issued later.

So, remember not to issue (distribute) all of the stock, because you may want to leave at least a few shares to issue later. You may want to issue some stock to a son or daughter entering the business, or to a new business partner. The main point to remember is that only **issued** shares count for ownership percentages. Take the following example for a corporation that has 1000 **authorized** (another word for available) shares of stock, and two owners.

Owner A is **issued** 100 shares 100/200=50% (Number owned divided by total issued.)

Owner B is **issued** 100 shares 100/200=50% (The same calculation)

The two owners own 50% of the corporation, as the 800 **un**issued shares are **not** considered in the calculation. 1000 authorized - 200 issued leaves 800 available for future use. Since only the 200 **issued** shares count for ownership, owners with 100 shares each own one half of the corporation. (One hundred is half of two hundred.)

To issue stock certificates to each shareholder, you must complete the face of the certificate, number the certificates sequentially, (01, 02, 03, 04, 05) and have the president and secretary sign the certificates on the lines at the bottom of the certificate. The large round area is where you will press the corporation's seal. Use the example stock certificate as a guide.

NOTE:
SEE THE IRS FORMS SECTION TO SEE IF YOU NEED TO FILE ANY IRS FORMS. YOUR TIME IS LIMITED TO A FIXED NUMBER OF DAYS TO FILE THESE FORMS, SO REVIEW THIS SECTION IMMEDIATELY **AFTER** INCORPORATING.

APPLICATION FOR RESERVATION OF CORPORATE NAME

Pursuant to Virginia Business Corporation Law, the undersigned individual submits the following application to reserve a corporate name:

1. The undersigned individual is the incorporator, and hereby applies for reservation of the following corporate name for the period of time allowed by Virginia Business Corporation Law.

2. The applicant is an individual.

3. The corporate name proposed for reservation meets the requirements of Virginia Business Corporation Law.

4. The name and street address of the applicant including the zip code is as follows:

____

____

____

________________________________.

5. The proposed name to be reserved is ________________________________.

____
Date

____
Signature of Applicant - Incorporator

____
Applicants Name(typed or printed)

SAMPLE
ARTICLES OF INCORPORATION

Pursuant to Virginia Business Corporation Law, the undersigned individual submits these Articles of Incorporation for the purpose of forming a corporation.

1. The name of the Corporation is A B C Inc. .

2. The complete street address and county of the Corporation's initial registered office,
AND the complete street address and county of the Corporation's principle office,
AND the complete street address and county of the Incorporator is

1234 Main Street Charlotte VA 23219 ,

County of Fairfax .

3. The person named in this article (3), is a Virginia resident, a director of the corporation, and is located at the address found in number 2. above. This person is the initial registered agent, AND the incorporator of the corporation, his/her name being William Brown .

4. The corporation is authorized to issue one thousand (1000) shares of no par value, common stock, with identical rights and privileges, the transfer of which is restricted according to the Bylaws. Preemptive rights to acquire additional shares are neither limited or denied. No shares have been issued.

5. The Corporation is organized for profit, with perpetual duration, beginning when these articles are filed. The corporation may engage in the transaction of any lawful business permitted by Virginia Business Corporation Law with the primary purpose of the corporation being

to publish books .

6. No Director shall be held liable to the corporation or its shareholders for monetary damages due to a breach of fiduciary duty, unless the breach is a result of self-dealing, intentional misconduct, or illegal actions.

7. The name(s) and address(es) of the Board of Directors, consisting of one individuals is/are:

William Brown	1234 Main Street Charlotte VA 23219

In witness whereof, the undersigned incorporator has executed these Articles of Incorporation on the date below:

Date	Signature of Incorporator	Name of Incorporator

ARTICLES OF INCORPORATION

Pursuant to Virginia Business Corporation Law, the undersigned individual submits these Articles of Incorporation for the purpose of forming a corporation.

1. The name of the Corporation is ____.

2. The complete street address and county of the Corporation's initial registered office,
AND the complete street address and county of the Corporation's principle office,
AND the complete street address and county of the Incorporator is

____,

County of ______________________.

3. The person named in this article (3), is a Virginia resident, a director of the corporation, and is located at the address found in number 2. above. This person is the initial registered agent, AND the incorporator of the corporation, his/her name being ______________________________________.

4. The corporation is authorized to issue one thousand (1000) shares of no par value, common stock, with identical rights and privileges, the transfer of which is restricted according to the Bylaws. Preemptive rights to acquire additional shares are neither limited or denied. No shares have been issued.

5. The Corporation is organized for profit, with perpetual duration, beginning when these articles are filed. The corporation may engage in the transaction of any lawful business permitted by Virginia Business Corporation Law, with the primary purpose of the corporation being

____.

6. No Director shall be held liable to the corporation or its shareholders for monetary damages due to a breach of fiduciary duty, unless the breach is a result of self-dealing, intentional misconduct, or illegal actions.

7. The name(s) and address(es) of the Board of Directors, consisting of ________ individuals is/are:

______________________	______________________________
______________________	______________________________
______________________	______________________________
______________________	______________________________
______________________	______________________________

In witness whereof, the undersigned incorporator has executed these Articles of Incorporation on the date below:

Date	Signature of Incorporator	Name of Incorporator

DIRECTORS CONSENT FOR ORGANIZATIONAL MATTERS

Pursuant to Virginia Business Corporation Law, and the bylaws, the Director(s) named below hereby consent to fulfilling the organizational requirements of Virginia Business Corporation Law without a meeting. By the affirmative vote of all Directors, the following actions shall be taken:

FIRST The individuals named in the Articles of Incorporation as Directors of the corporation, will be Directors of the Corporation until the next annual shareholders meeting.

SECOND As their responsibilities are outlined in the Corporation Bylaws, the following individuals shall be Officers and employees of the Corporation with their respective titles below their name, and their agreed upon annual salary to the right. These individuals will be officers until the next annual shareholder's meeting.

______________________	__________
President	President's Salary
______________________	__________
Vice-President	Vice-Pres. Salary
______________________	__________
Secretary	Secretary's Salary
______________________	__________
Treasurer	Treasurer's Salary

THIRD The Bylaws as contained in the book of CORPORATE RECORDS shall be the Bylaws of the Corporation and are hereby adopted by the shareholders and directors.

FOURTH The incorporator's duties are complete, and the incorporator is hereby released. Any and all requirements of Virginia Business Corporation Law shall be, and are hereby met.

		yes
Date of Signatures	Director	Vote
		yes
	Director	Vote
		yes
	Director	Vote
		yes
	Director	Vote
		yes
SECRETARY	Director	Vote

DIRECTORS CONSENT TO ISSUE STOCK OF THE CORPORATION

Pursuant to Virginia Business Corporation Law, the Directors of the Corporation hereby consent to approving actions of the Corporation without a meeting. This consent has the same effect as a meeting vote. By the affirmative vote of a majority of the Directors, as evidenced by the signatures below, the following actions shall be taken:

FIRST The time has come to issue the stock of the Corporation under the direction of the Board of Directors. The individuals listed below are those who desire to acquire said stocks. Next to the individuals name is the number of shares they are acquiring, the percentage ownership of the Corporation that number of shares represents, and the payment given for the shares, respectively. Note that the Board of Directors has approved the amount of payment given for the stock, and if there is not enough space provided below to describe said payment, it will be listed in the stock transfer ledger. Stock certificates may be issued as evidence of stock ownership, and will be signed by the Corporation President and Secretary. Additional stockholders are listed on the reverse. Also, the stock shall qualify for, and may be treated as IRS § 1244 stock.

Name	No. of Shares	% Ownership	Payment Given
Name	No. of Shares	% Ownership	Payment Given
Name	No. of Shares	% Ownership	Payment Given
Name	No. of Shares	% Ownership	Payment Given
Name	No. of Shares	% Ownership	Payment Given

yes

Date of Signatures — Director — Vote

yes

Director — Vote

yes

Director — Vote

yes

Director — Vote

yes

SECRETARY — Director — Vote

NUMBER 01

SHARES 100

ABC INC.

A VIRGINIA CORPORATION - RESTRICTED STOCK - TOTAL AUTHORIZED ISSUE IS 1000 SHARES WITHOUT PAR VALUE

This Certifies that WILLIAM BROWN is the registered holder of ONE HUNDRED Shares

transferable only on the books of the Corporation by the holder hereof in person or by Attorney upon surrender of this Certificate properly endorsed.

In Witness Whereof, the said Corporation has caused this Certificate to be signed by its duly authorized officers and its Corporate Seal to be hereunto affixed this 1st day of May A.D. 19 91

Secretary

Pres.

INCORPORATED UNDER THE LAWS OF

NUMBER

SHARES

A VIRGINIA CORPORATION TOTAL AUTHORIZED ISSUE IS 1000 SHARES WITHOUT PAR VALUE RESTRICTED STOCK

This Certifies that ______________________ is the registered holder of ______________________ Shares

transferable only on the books of the Corporation by the holder hereof in person or by Attorney upon surrender of this Certificate properly endorsed.

IN WITNESS WHEREOF, the said Corporation has caused this Certificate to be signed by its duly authorized officers and its Corporate Seal to be hereunto affixed this ______ day of ______ A.D. 19__

CERTIFICATE FOR

SHARES

OF

ISSUED TO

DATED

For Value Received, ______ *hereby sell, assign and transfer unto* ______________________________

______________________________ *Shares represented by the within Certificate, and do hereby irrevocably constitute and appoint*

______________________________ *Attorney to transfer the said Shares on the books of the within named Corporation with full power of substitution in the premises.*

Dated ______________ *19* ____

In presence of

____

____

NOTICE. THE SIGNATURE OF THIS ASSIGNMENT MUST CORRESPOND WITH THE NAME AS WRITTEN UPON THE FACE OF THE CERTIFICATE, IN EVERY PARTICULAR, WITHOUT ALTERATION OR ENLARGEMENT, OR ANY CHANGE WHATEVER.

INCORPORATED UNDER THE LAWS OF

NUMBER

SHARES

A VIRGINIA CORPORATION   TOTAL AUTHORIZED ISSUE IS 1000 SHARES WITHOUT PAR VALUE   RESTRICTED STOCK

This Certifies that ______________________________ is the registered holder of ______________________________ Shares

transferable only on the books of the Corporation by the holder hereof in person or by Attorney upon surrender of this Certificate properly endorsed.

IN WITNESS WHEREOF, the said Corporation has caused this Certificate to be signed by its duly authorized officers and its Corporate Seal to be hereunto affixed this ____________ day of ____________ A.D. 19

CERTIFICATE FOR

SHARES

OF

ISSUED TO

DATED

For Value Received, ______ *hereby sell, assign and transfer unto* ____

____ *Shares represented by the within Certificate, and do hereby irrevocably constitute and appoint*

____ *Attorney to transfer the said Shares on the books of the within named Corporation with full power of substitution in the premises.*

Dated ________________ *19* ____

In presence of

________________________ ________________________

NOTICE. THE SIGNATURE OF THIS ASSIGNMENT MUST CORRESPOND WITH THE NAME AS WRITTEN UPON THE FACE OF THE CERTIFICATE, IN EVERY PARTICULAR, WITHOUT ALTERATION OR ENLARGEMENT, OR ANY CHANGE WHATEVER.

INCORPORATED UNDER THE LAWS OF

NUMBER

SHARES

A VIRGINIA CORPORATION TOTAL AUTHORIZED ISSUE IS 1000 SHARES WITHOUT PAR VALUE RESTRICTED STOCK

This Certifies that ______________________________ is the registered holder of ______________________________ Shares

transferable only on the books of the Corporation by the holder hereof in person or by Attorney upon surrender of this Certificate properly endorsed.

In Witness Whereof, the said Corporation has caused this Certificate to be signed by its duly authorized officers and its Corporate Seal to be hereunto affixed this ________ day of ________ A.D. 19 ____

For Value Received, ______ hereby sell, assign and transfer unto ______________________________

______________________________ Shares represented by the within Certificate, and do hereby irrevocably constitute and appoint

______________________________ Attorney to transfer the said Shares on the books of the within named Corporation with full power of substitution in the premises.

Dated ______________ 19____

In presence of

____

____

NOTICE. THE SIGNATURE OF THIS ASSIGNMENT MUST CORRESPOND WITH THE NAME AS WRITTEN UPON THE FACE OF THE CERTIFICATE, IN EVERY PARTICULAR, WITHOUT ALTERATION OR ENLARGEMENT, OR ANY CHANGE WHATEVER.

INCORPORATED UNDER THE LAWS OF

NUMBER

SHARES

A VIRGINIA CORPORATION TOTAL AUTHORIZED ISSUE IS 1000 SHARES WITHOUT PAR VALUE RESTRICTED STOCK

This Certifies that ______________________________ is the registered holder of ______________________________ Shares

transferable only on the books of the Corporation by the holder hereof in person or by Attorney upon surrender of this Certificate properly endorsed.

IN WITNESS WHEREOF, the said Corporation has caused this Certificate to be signed by its duly authorized officers and its Corporate Seal to be hereunto affixed this ________ day of ________ A.D. 19____

For Value Received, ______ *hereby sell, assign and transfer*
unto ______________________________

______________________________ *Shares*
represented by the within Certificate, and do hereby
irrevocably constitute and appoint
______________________________ *Attorney*
to transfer the said Shares on the books of the within named
Corporation with full power of substitution in the premises.
Dated ______________ *19* ____

In presence of

______________________________ ______________________________

NOTICE. THE SIGNATURE OF THIS ASSIGNMENT MUST CORRESPOND WITH THE NAME AS WRITTEN UPON THE FACE OF THE CERTIFICATE, IN EVERY PARTICULAR, WITHOUT ALTERATION OR ENLARGEMENT, OR ANY CHANGE WHATEVER.

CERTIFICATE
FOR
______
SHARES

OF

ISSUED TO
____
DATED
____

INCORPORATED UNDER THE LAWS OF

NUMBER

SHARES

A VIRGINIA CORPORATION TOTAL AUTHORIZED ISSUE IS 1000 SHARES WITHOUT PAR VALUE RESTRICTED STOCK

This Certifies that ______________________ is the registered holder of ______________________ Shares

transferable only on the books of the Corporation by the holder hereof in person or by Attorney upon surrender of this Certificate properly endorsed.

IN WITNESS WHEREOF, the said Corporation has caused this Certificate to be signed by its duly authorized officers and its Corporate Seal to be hereunto affixed this ________ day of ________ A.D. 19 ____

For Value Received, ____ hereby sell, assign and transfer unto ________________________

________________________ Shares represented by the within Certificate, and do hereby irrevocably constitute and appoint

________________________ Attorney to transfer the said Shares on the books of the within named Corporation with full power of substitution in the premises.

Dated ________________ 19___

In presence of

____

____

NOTICE. THE SIGNATURE OF THIS ASSIGNMENT MUST CORRESPOND WITH THE NAME AS WRITTEN UPON THE FACE OF THE CERTIFICATE, IN EVERY PARTICULAR, WITHOUT ALTERATION OR ENLARGEMENT OR ANY CHANGE WHATEVER.

SECTION 3
IRS FORMS

INSTRUCTIONS FOR IRS FORMS

On the next few pages, you will find an IRS form, it's instructions, and a directors consent. The form is called a 2553, and is used to tell the IRS (if you desire) that you wish to be classified as a "small business corporation" according to their rules. The major difference between a regular, or "C" corporation, and the small business or "S" corporation, is that a C corporation is responsible for its own income tax, and the S corporation is not liable for Federal income tax.

The S corporation taxes, if any, are paid by its stockholders on their personal returns. You might say this sounds like a bad deal until you consider that many S corporations "lose" money, or are made to lose money, in which case the stockholder gets a deduction on his personal return. If you had a C corporation, the loss would be the corporation's, and you would not benefit from it. Conversely, if the C corporation did not pay any dividends, you would have no tax liability from the corporation's income.

Since many chapters could be devoted to this subject, a separate subject from this manual, we will simply say that you need to discuss it with your CPA, or financial advisor. However, we will add that most corporations with less than 15 stockholders are "S" corporations.

If you do elect to be treated as an S corporation, you will need to complete the accompanying consent for corporate record keeping. The consent shows that the directors officially approved the action. **Do not send the <u>consent</u> to the IRS.**

PLEASE NOTE THAT A 2553 ELECTION HAS NOTHING TO DO WITH THE STATE. ELECTING S CORPORATION STATUS SIMPLY TELLS THE IRS HOW YOU WANT TO BE CLASSIFIED FOR CORPORATE INCOME TAX REPORTING. DO NOT SEND ANY OF THESE IRS FORMS TO THE CORPORATION COMMISSION.

Form **2553**
(Rev. October 1989)
Department of the Treasury
Internal Revenue Service

Election by a Small Business Corporation

(Under section 1362 of the Internal Revenue Code)
► For Paperwork Reduction Act Notice, see page 1 of instructions.
► See separate instructions.

OMB No. 1545-0146
Expires 2-28-91

Notes: 1. *This election, to be treated as an "S corporation," can be accepted only if all the tests in General Instruction B are met; all signatures in Parts I and III are originals (no photocopies); and the exact name and address of the corporation and other required form information are provided.*
2. *Do not file Form 1120S until you are notified that your election is accepted. See instruction E.*

Part I Election Information

Please Type or Print

Name of corporation (see instructions)	**A Employer identification number** (see instructions)	**B** Principal business activity and principal product or service (see instructions)
Number and street	**C** Name and telephone number of corporate officer or legal representative who may be called for information	
City or town, state, and ZIP code	**D** Election is to be effective for tax year beginning (month, day, year)	

E (1) Is the corporation the outgrowth or continuation of any form of predecessor? ☐ **Yes** ☐ **No**
If "Yes," state name of predecessor, type of organization, and period of its existence ► ....
(2) Check here ☐ if the corporation has changed its name or address since applying for the employer identification number shown in item A above.

F Date of incorporation

G State of incorporation

H If this election takes effect for the first tax year the corporation exists, enter month, day, and year of the **earliest** of the following: (1) date the corporation first had shareholders, (2) date the corporation first had assets, or (3) date the corporation began doing business. ►

I Selected tax year: Annual return will be filed for tax year ending (month and day) ► ....
See instructions before entering your tax year. If the tax year ends on any date other than December 31, except for an automatic 52–53-week tax year ending with reference to the month of December, you must complete Part II on the back. If the date you enter in item I is the ending date of an automatic 52–53-week tax year, write "52–53-week year" to the right of the date. See instructions.

J Name of each shareholder, person having a community property interest in the corporation's stock, and each tenant in common, joint tenant, and tenant by the entirety. (A husband and wife (and their estates) are counted as one shareholder in determining the number of shareholders without regard to the manner in which the stock is owned.)	**K** Shareholders' Consent Statement. We, the undersigned shareholders, consent to the corporation's election to be treated as an "S corporation" under section 1362(a). (Shareholders sign and date below.)*	**L** Stock owned		**M** Social security number or employer identification number (see instructions)	**N** Shareholder's tax year ends (month and day)
		Number of shares	Dates acquired		

*For this election to be valid, the consent of each shareholder, person having a community property interest in the corporation's stock, and each tenant in common, joint tenant, and tenant by the entirety must either appear above or be attached to this form. (See instructions for Column K, if continuation sheet or a separate consent statement is needed.)

Under penalties of perjury, I declare that I have examined this election, including accompanying schedules and statements, and to the best of my knowledge and belief, it is true, correct, and complete.

Signature and Title of Officer ► **Date ►**

See Parts II and III on back.

Part II Selection of Fiscal Tax Year (All corporations using this Part must complete item O and one of items P, Q, or R.) (See instructions for information about a user fee, if applicable, required attachments, and other details.)

O Check the applicable box below to indicate whether the corporation is:

☐ A new corporation adopting the tax year entered in item I, Part I.

☐ An existing corporation retaining the tax year entered in item I, Part I.

☐ An existing corporation changing to the tax year entered in item I, Part I.

P Check the applicable box below to indicate the representation statement the corporation is making as required under section 4 of Rev. Proc. 87-32, 1987-2 C.B. 396.

☐ Under penalties of perjury, I represent that shareholders holding more than half of the shares of the stock (as of the first day of the tax year to which the request relates) of the corporation have the same tax year or are concurrently changing to the tax year that the corporation adopts, retains, or changes to per item I, Part I. I also represent that the corporation is not described in section 3.01(2) of Rev. Proc. 87-32.

☐ Under penalties of perjury, I represent that the corporation is retaining or changing to a tax year that coincides with its natural business year as defined in section 4.01(1) of Rev. Proc. 87-32 and as verified by its satisfaction of the requirements of section 4.02(1) of Rev. Proc. 87-32. In addition, if the corporation is changing to a natural business year as defined in section 4.01(1), I further represent that such tax year results in less deferral of income to the owners than the corporation's present tax year. I also represent that the corporation is not described in section 3.01(2) of Rev. Proc. 87-32. (See instructions for attachments required by section 4.03(3) of Rev. Proc. 87-32.)

Note: *If you do not use item P and the corporation wants a fiscal tax year, complete either item Q or R below. Item Q is used to request a fiscal tax year based on business purpose and to make a back-up section 444 election. Item R is used to make a regular section 444 election.*

Q Business Purpose—To request a fiscal tax year based on busines purpose, you must check box Q1. You may also check box Q2 and/or box Q3.

1. Check here ☐ if the fiscal year entered in item I, Part I, is requested under the provisions of section 6.03 of Rev. Proc. 87-32. Attach to Form 2553 a statement and other necessary information pursuant to the ruling request requirements of Rev. Proc. 89-1, 1989-1 I.R.B. 8. The statement must include the business purpose for the desired fiscal year.

2. Check here ☐ to show that the corporation intends to make a back-up section 444 election in the event the corporation's business purpose request is not approved by the IRS.

3. Check here ☐ to show that the corporation agrees to adopt or change to a tax year ending December 31 if necessary for the IRS to accept this election for S corporation status in the event: (1) the corporation's business purpose request is not approved and the corporation makes a back-up section 444 election, but is ultimately not qualified to make a section 444 election, or (2) the corporation's business purpose request is not approved and the corporation did not make a back-up section 444 election.

R Section 444 Election—You must check box R1 and you may also check box R2.

1. Check here ☐ to show the corporation will make, if qualified, a section 444 election to have the fiscal tax year shown in item I, Part I. To make the election, you must complete **Form 8716,** Election To Have a Tax Year Other Than a Required Tax Year, and either attach it to Form 2553 or file it in accordance with the instructions for Form 8716.

2. Check here ☐ to show that the corporation agrees to adopt or change to a tax year ending December 31 if necessary for the IRS to accept this election for S corporation status in the event the corporation is ultimately not qualified to make a section 444 election.

Part III Qualified Subchapter S Trust (QSST) Election Under Section 1361(d)(2)**

Income beneficiary's name and address	Taxpayer identification number
Trust's name and address	Taxpayer identification number

Date on which stock of the corporation was transferred to the trust (month, day, year) ▶

In order for the trust named above to be a QSST and thus a qualifying shareholder of the S corporation for which this Form 2553 is filed, I hereby make the election under section 1361(d)(2). Under penalties of perjury, I certify that the trust meets the definition requirements of section 1361(d)(3) and that all other information provided in Part III is true, correct, and complete.

Signature of income beneficiary or signature and title of legal representative or other qualified person making the election — Date

**Use of Part III to make the QSST election may be made only if stock of the corporation has been transferred to the trust on or before the date on which the corporation makes its election to be an S corporation. The QSST election must be made and filed separately if stock of the corporation is transferred to the trust after the date on which the corporation makes the S election.

☆ U.S. Government Printing Office:1989-261-151/00018

Department of the Treasury
Internal Revenue Service

Instructions for Form 2553

(Revised October 1989)

Election by a Small Business Corporation

(Section references are to the Internal Revenue Code unless otherwise noted.)

Paperwork Reduction Act Notice.—We ask for this information to carry out the Internal Revenue laws of the United States. We need it to insure that you are complying with these laws and to allow us to figure and collect the right amount of tax. You are required to give us this information.

The time needed to complete and file this form will vary depending on individual circumstances. The estimated average time is:

Recordkeeping . . . . 6 hrs., 42 min.

Learning about the law or the form . . . . 3 hrs., 16 min.

Preparing, copying, assembling, and sending the form to IRS . . . . 3 hrs., 32 min.

If you have comments concerning the accuracy of these time estimates or suggestions for making this form more simple, we would be happy to hear from you. You can write to the **Internal Revenue Service**, Washington, DC 20224, Attention: IRS Reports Clearance Officer, T:FP; or the **Office of Management and Budget**, Paperwork Reduction Project (1545-0146), Washington, DC 20503.

General Instructions

A. Purpose.—To elect to be treated as an "S Corporation," a corporation must file Form 2553. The election permits the income of the S corporation to be taxed to the shareholders of the corporation, except as provided in Subchapter S of the Code.

B. Who May Elect.—Your corporation may make the election to be treated as an S corporation only if it meets all of the following tests:

1. It is a domestic corporation.
2. It has no more than 35 shareholders. A husband and wife (and their estates) are treated as one shareholder for this requirement. All other persons are treated as separate shareholders.
3. It has only individuals, estates, or certain trusts as shareholders. See the instructions for Part III regarding qualified subchapter S trusts.
4. It has no nonresident alien shareholders.
5. It has only one class of stock. See sections 1361(c)(4) and (5) for additional details.
6. It is not an ineligible corporation as defined in section 1361(b)(2).
7. It has a permitted tax year as required by section 1378 or makes a section 444 election to have a tax year other than a permitted tax year. Section 1378 defines a permitted tax year as a tax year ending December 31, or any other tax year for which the corporation establishes a business purpose to the satisfaction of the IRS. See the instructions for Part II for details on making a section 444 election.
8. Each shareholder consents as explained in the instructions for Column K.

See sections 1361, 1362, and 1378 for additional information on the above tests.

C. Where To File.—File this election with the Internal Revenue Service Center where the corporation will file **Form 1120S**, U.S. Income Tax Return for an S Corporation. See the Instructions for Form 1120S for Service Center addresses.

D. When To Make the Election.—Complete Form 2553 and file it either: (1) at any time during that portion of the first tax year the election is to take effect which occurs before the 16th day of the third month of that tax year (if the tax year has 2½ months or less, and the election is made not later than 2 months and 15 days after the first day of the tax year, it shall be treated as timely made during such year), or (2) in the tax year before the first tax year it is to take effect. An election made by a small business corporation after the 15th day of the third month but before the end of the tax year is treated as made for the next year. For example, if a calendar tax year corporation makes the election in April 1988, it is effective for the corporation's 1989 calendar tax year. See section 1362(b) for more information.

E. Acceptance or Non-Acceptance of Election.—The Service Center will notify you if your election is accepted and when it will take effect. You should generally receive a determination on your election within 60 days after you have filed Form 2553. If the Q1 box in Part II is checked on page 2, the corporation will receive a ruling letter from IRS in Washington, DC, which approves or denies the selected tax year. When Item Q1 is checked, it will generally take an additional 90 days for the Form 2553 to be accepted.

Do not file Form 1120S until you are notified that your election is accepted. If you are now required to file **Form 1120**, U.S. Corporation Income Tax Return, or any other applicable tax return, continue filing it until your election takes effect.

You will also be notified if your election is not accepted.

Care should be exercised to ensure that the election is received by the Internal Revenue Service. If you are not notified of acceptance or nonacceptance of your election within 3 months of date of filing (date mailed), or within 6 months if Part II, Item Q1, is checked, you should take follow-up action by corresponding with the Service Center where the election was filed. If filing of Form 2553 is questioned by IRS, an acceptable proof of filing is: (1) certified receipt (timely filed); (2) Form 2553 with accepted stamp; (3) Form 2553 with stamped IRS received date; or (4) IRS letter stating that Form 2553 had been accepted.

F. End of Election.—Once the election is made, it stays in effect for all years until it is terminated. During the 5 years after the election is terminated under section 1362(d), the corporation can make another election on Form 2553 only if the Commissioner consents. See section 1362(g) for more information. See sections 1362(d), (e), and (f) for rules regarding termination of election.

G. User Fee.—Corporations filing Form 2553 and requesting a fiscal year under section 6.03 of Revenue Procedure 87-32, 1987-2 C.B. 396, must pay a user fee ($150 when these instructions were revised). Payment of the fee (check or money order) should not be made with or attached to Form 2553 when it is filed. The Service Center sends Form 2553 to the IRS in Washington, DC, who, in turn, notifies the taxpayer that the fee is due. See Revenue Procedure 89-4, 1989-3 I.R.B. 18.

Specific Instructions

Part I.—Part I must be completed by all corporations.

Name and Address of Corporation.—If the corporation's mailing address is the same as someone else's, such as a shareholder's, please enter this person's name below the name of the corporation. Enter the true corporate name as set forth in the corporate charter or other legal document creating it. If the corporation has changed its name or address since applying for its EIN (filing Form SS-4), be sure to check the box in item E(2) of Part I.

A. Employer Identification Number.—If you have applied for an employer identification number (EIN) but have not received it, enter "applied for." If the corporation does not have an EIN, you should apply for one on **Form SS-4**, Application for Employer Identification Number, available from most IRS or Social Security Administration offices. Send Form SS-4 to the IRS Service Center where Form 1120S will be filed.

B. Principal Business Activity and Principal Product or Service.—Use the Codes for Principal Business Activity contained in the Instructions for Form 1120S. Your principal business activity is the one that accounts for the largest percentage of total receipts. Total receipts are gross receipts plus all other income.

Also state the principal product or service. For example, if the principal business activity is "grain mill products," the principal product or service may be "cereal preparation."

C. Name and Telephone Number.—Enter the name and telephone number (area code and seven digit number) of a corporate officer or legal representative of the corporation who IRS may contact to resolve questions (or obtain additional information) that may arise when the corporation's Form 2553 is reviewed.

D. Effective Date of Election.—Enter the beginning effective date (month, day, year) of the tax year that you have requested for the S corporation. Generally, this will be the beginning date of the tax year for which the ending effective date is shown in item I, Part I. For a new corporation (first year the corporation exists) it will generally be the date shown in item H, Part I. The tax year of a new corporation starts on the date that it has shareholders, acquires assets, or begins doing business, whichever happens first. If the effective date for item D for a newly formed corporation is later than the date in item H, the corporation should file Form 1120, or Form 1120A, for the tax period between these dates.

I. Selected Tax Year.—If a corporation selects a tax year ending other than December 31 (excluding a 52-53-week tax year with reference to the month of December), the corporation must complete Part II in addition to Part I.

Temporary Regulations section 1.441-2T(e)(3) grants automatic approval to the S corporation to use a 52-53-week tax year with reference to the month of December.

Column K. Shareholders' consent statement.—Each shareholder who owns (or is deemed to own) stock at the time the election is made must consent to the election. If the election is made during the corporation's first tax year for which it is effective, any person who held stock at any time during the portion of that year which occurs before the time the election is made, must consent to the election although the person may have sold or transferred his or her stock before the election is made. Each shareholder consents by signing and dating in column K or signing and dating a separate consent statement described below. If stock is owned by a trust that is a qualified shareholder, the deemed owner of the trust must consent. See section 1361(c)(2) for details regarding qualified trusts that may be shareholders and rules on determining who is the deemed owner of the trust.

An election made during the first 2½ months of the tax year is considered made for the following tax year if one or more of the persons who held stock in the corporation during such tax year and before the election was made did not consent to the election. See section 1362(b)(2).

If a husband and wife have a community interest in the stock or in the income from it, both must consent. Each tenant in common, joint tenant, and tenant by the entirety also must consent.

A minor's consent is made by the minor or the legal representative of the minor, or by a natural or adoptive parent of the minor if no legal representative has been appointed. The consent of an estate is made by an executor or administrator.

Continuation sheet or separate consent statement.—If you need a continuation sheet or use a separate consent statement, attach it to Form 2553. The separate consent statement must contain the name, address, and employer identification number of the corporation and the shareholder information requested in columns J through N of Part I.

If you wish, you may combine all the shareholders' consents in one statement.

Column L.—Enter the number of shares of stock each shareholder owns and the dates the stock was acquired. If the election is made during the corporation's first tax year for which it is effective, do not list the shares of stock for those shareholders who sold or transferred all of their stock before the election was made. However, these shareholders must still consent to the election for it to be effective for the tax year.

Column M.—Enter the social security number for shareholders who are individuals. Enter the employer identification number for estates. Enter the social security number or employer identification number for shareholders that are qualified trusts.

Column N.—Enter the month and day that each shareholder's tax year ends. If a shareholder is changing his or her tax year, enter the tax year the shareholder is changing to. If a shareholder is changing his or her tax year, an explanation should be attached to Form 2553 indicating the present tax year and the basis for the change (e.g., automatic revenue procedure or letter ruling request).

If the election is made during the corporation's first tax year for which it is effective, you do not have to enter the tax year of shareholders who sold or transferred all of their stock before the election was made but who still must consent to the election for it to be effective for the tax year.

Signature.—Form 2553 must be signed by the president, treasurer, assistant treasurer, chief accounting officer, or other corporate officer (such as tax officer) authorized to sign.

Part II

Item P.—Item P is completed by a corporation that selects a fiscal year, and that qualifies under section 4.01(1) or 4.01(2) of Revenue Procedure 87-32, 1987-2 C.B. 396. In addition, if the corporation selects a fiscal year that qualifies under section 4.01(1), then it must attach a statement to Form 2553, showing the amount of gross receipts for the most recent 47 months (show each month separately) as required by section 4.03(3)(b) of the revenue procedure. Sections 4.01(1) and 4.01(2) provide for expeditious approval of certain corporations' requests to adopt, retain, or change to a fiscal year. The representation statements highlight the requests provided for in section 4 of the revenue procedure. A corporation adopting, retaining, or changing its accounting period under the procedure must comply with all applicable conditions of the procedure.

Form 1128, Application for Change in Accounting Period, should not be used to request a tax year for or during the 1st year the corporation elects to be an S corporation.

Item Q.—Item Q is completed as follows:

Box Q1.—The corporation checks box Q1 to make a request as specified in section 6.03 of Revenue Procedure 87-32. The taxpayer must attach a statement to Form 2553 pursuant to the ruling request requirements of Revenue Procedure 89-1, 1989-1 I.R.B. 8. (Changes to this revenue procedure are usually incorporated annually into a new revenue procedure as the first revenue procedure of the year.) The statement must show the business purpose for the desired tax year. See Revenue Ruling 87-57, 1987-2 C.B. 117, for examples of business purpose. Also, submit figures showing monthly gross receipts from sales or services (and monthly inventory figures, if applicable) for the 36 months immediately preceding the effective date of the Form 2553. If the corporation has been in existence for less than 36 months, submit figures for the period of existence.

Box Q2.—The corporation checks box Q2 to show its intention to make a back-up section 444 election. The back-up section 444 election is made in addition to the request for a fiscal year based on business purpose. The back-up election applies in the event the IRS does not approve the corporation's request for a tax year based on business purpose. **Caution: If the corporation makes a back-up section 444 election for which it is qualified, then the election must be exercised in the event the business purpose request is denied.**

Under certain circumstances, the tax year requested under the section 444 back-up election may be different than the tax year requested under business purpose. See the instructions for Form 8716 for details on making a back-up section 444 election.

Box Q3.—The corporation checks box Q3 to make a calendar year back-up election. The calendar year back-up election applies if: (a) the corporation's business purpose request is denied, or (b) the business purpose request was denied and the section 444 back-up election was made, but later the corporation was not eligible to make the election. In certain cases, the corporation will not be eligible to make the section 444 election when it becomes a member of a tiered structure.

Item R.—Item R is completed as follows:

Box R1.—The corporation checks box R1 to show that it is making or intends to make the section 444 election. The corporation makes the election when filing Form 2553 by completing Form 8716 and attaching it to Form 2553. Form 8716 can also be completed and filed after Form 2553 is filed. See the instructions for Form 8716 for details on filing Form 8716.

Box R2.—The corporation checks box R2 to make a back-up calendar year election.

If the corporation is not qualified to make the section 444 election after making the item Q2 section 444 back-up election or indicating its intention to make the election in item R1, and therefore it later files a calendar year return, it should write "Section 444 Election Not Made" in the top left corner of the 1st calendar year Form 1120S it files.

Part III

Certain Qualified Subchapter S Trusts (QSSTs) may make the QSST election required by section 1361(d)(2) in Part III. Part III may be used to make the QSST election only if corporate stock has been transferred to the trust on or before the date on which the corporation makes its election to be an S corporation. However, a statement can be used in lieu of Part III to make the election.

Note: *Part III may be used only in conjunction with making the Part I election (i.e., Form 2553 cannot be filed with only Part III being completed).*

The deemed owner of the QSST must also consent to the S corporation election in column K, page 1, of Form 2553. See section 1361(c)(2).

* U.S. Government Printing Office: 1989-261-151/00021

WRITTEN CONSENT TO CORPORATE ACTION

Pursuant to Virginia Business Corporation Law, the Directors of the Corporation hereby consent to approving actions of the Corporation without a meeting. This consent has the same effect as a meeting vote. By the affirmative vote of a majority of the Directors, as evidenced by the signatures below, the following actions shall be taken:

FIRST It is decided that in the best interest of the stockholders the Corporation should elect federal taxation treatment under Subchapter S of the Internal Revenue Code as provided by the Internal Revenue Service, which would allow the Corporation to be taxed as a partnership, with the income or loss of the Corporation "passing through" to the stockholders. Consent and agreement of the stockholders will be evidenced by their signatures on Federal Tax Form Number 2553, a copy of which shall be included in the records of the Corporation. By electing tax treatment under Subchapter S, the Corporation will be required to use a calendar year with the tax year ending December 31, of each year.

yes

Date of Signatures ______________ Director ______________________________ Vote

yes

Director ______________________________ Vote

yes

Director ______________________________ Vote

yes

Director ______________________________ Vote

yes

Director ______________________________ Vote

SECRETARY ______________________________

Name of Corporation ______________________________

SECTION 4
BYLAWS

INSTRUCTIONS FOR BYLAWS

The bylaws of the corporation are the rules by which it operates. Just as a city has laws for its citizens, a corporation has laws for its shareholders, directors, and officers. The only thing you'll need to do with the bylaws is read them, and become familiar with <u>your</u> corporate rules. Become especially familiar with the procedure a shareholder must follow before selling any stock as outlined in ARTICLE FOUR.

Also, note in ARTICLE FIVE you must complete the time and date of the annual meeting of the corporation. This can be any date and time that is convenient for you that allows enough time to prepare financial reports for the year just ended. Remember, the minutes of the annual shareholders meeting have already been prepared, so all you really need to do is sign and date them. Most people never really have an annual shareholder's meeting, they just sign the minutes and file them away.

BYLAWS
OF

The following shall be known as the bylaws of the Corporation, the bylaws being rules of self government of the Corporation. These bylaws are the set of rules by which the Corporation operates on a daily basis and settles disputes that may arise from time to time; and they are binding on all those associated with the Corporation either now, or in the future. If the Bylaws are found to be inconsistent with Virginia Law, then Virginia Law will be supreme.

ARTICLE ONE
PURPOSE

The Corporation may take advantage of the rights granted to it by Virginia State law, and engage in any business allowed by Virginia Business Corporation Law.

ARTICLE TWO
DURATION

The Corporation has perpetual duration and succession in its corporate name and will exist until such time that the Board of Directors elects to end its existence.

ARTICLE THREE
POWERS

The Corporation has the powers given by Virginia Business Corporation Law, to do all things necessary or practical to carry out its business and affairs including without limitation, the power to sue, make contracts, deal in property of any kind, make investments, borrow or lend money, be a part of another entity, or conduct its business in any way allowed by the laws of this State.

ARTICLE FOUR
SHARES

The shares of the Corporation will be common stock, with full voting rights and identical rights and privileges, with no par value. The issuance of shares will be governed by the Board of Directors, as will be the consideration to be paid for the shares, which will meet the requirements of Virginia Business Corporation Law. The Corporation through its Board of Directors may issue fractional shares, acquire its own shares, declare and pay cash or stock dividends, or issue certificates.

In order to insure the continued existence of the Corporation, the transfer of shares of the Corporation to any individual or other entity will be restricted in the manner described herein. No shares may be transferred on the books of the Corporation unless the number of shares are first offered to the Corporation, and then to the other shareholders on a right of first refusal basis, the corporation having first option. This option to purchase the stock will expire in thirty (30) days from when offered. If the option is not exercised within the stated period, the Shareholder may dispose of the shares in any manner he wishes. The share certificates shall bear the following notice: RESTRICTED STOCK

ARTICLE FIVE
MEETINGS

REGULAR MEETINGS The Corporation may hold any number of meetings to conduct its business. At a minimum, it will hold an annual Shareholders' meeting at which the Directors will review with the Shareholders the operating results of the Corporation for the prior year, hold elections for Directors, and conduct any other business that may be necessary at that time. The place and time for the annual Shareholders' meeting will be at the offices of the Corporation on the ____________ day of____________________, at the time of ____________, each year. The Secretary will give proper notice to the Shareholders as may be required by law, however that notice may be waived by the Shareholder by submitting a signed waiver either before or after the meeting, or by his attendance at the meeting. Meetings may be held in or out of this State. Minutes must be taken by the Secretary for inclusion in the Corporate Records.

SPECIAL (NON REGULAR) MEETINGS The Corporation may hold meetings from time to time at such times and places that may be convenient. These meetings may be Directors meetings or Shareholder meetings or combined Director and Shareholder meetings. Special <u>Shareholder</u> meetings may be called by The Board of Directors or demanded in writing by the holders of Ten percent or more shares. Special <u>Director</u> meetings may be called by the Chairman, the President, or any two Directors. The Corporate Secretary will give proper notice as may be required by law, however that notice may be waived by the individual by submitting a signed waiver either before or after the meeting, or by his attendance at the meeting. Meetings may be held in or out of this State. Minutes must be taken by the Secretary for inclusion in the Corporate Records.

ARTICLE SIX
VOTING

From time to time it may be necessary for a Director or Shareholder to vote on issues brought before a meeting. No voting may take place at a meeting unless there is a quorum present. That is, a quorum of Directors must be present at a meeting before any Director may vote, and likewise a quorum of Shareholders must be present at a meeting before any Shareholder may vote. A quorum of Directors at a meeting is defined as a majority of the number of Directors. A quorum of Shareholders at a meeting is defined as a majority of the shares entitled to vote. If a quorum is present at a meeting, action on a matter may be passed if the number of votes favoring the action is cast by a majority. For voting purposes, a Director may cast one vote, and a Shareholder may cast one vote for each share held. A Shareholder may vote in person or by proxy.

ARTICLE SEVEN
ACTION WITHOUT MEETING

Directors or Shareholders may approve actions without a formal meeting if all entitled to vote on a matter consent to taking such action without a meeting. A majority still is required to pass actions without a meeting. The action must be evidenced by a written consent describing the action taken, signed by the Directors or Shareholders (depending on which group is taking the action) indicating each signer's vote or abstention on the matter, and it must be delivered to the Corporate Secretary for inclusion with the Corporate Records.

ARTICLE EIGHT
DIRECTORS

All corporate powers will be exercised by, or under the authority of, and the business affairs of the Corporation managed under the direction of, its Board of Directors. The Board may consist of one or more individuals, who need not need be Shareholders or residents of this state. The terms of the initial Directors or or subsequently elected Directors will end at the next Shareholders' meeting following their election, at which time new Directors will be elected or the current Directors will be reelected. A director may resign at any time by delivering a written notice to the Corporation. A Director may be removed at any time with or without cause if the number of votes cast to remove him exceeds the number of votes cast not to remove him. Vacancies on the Board will be filled by the Shareholders in the manner described above.

The Directors of the Corporation are not liable to either the Corporation or its Shareholders for monetary damages for a breach of fiduciary duties unless the breach involves disloyalty to the Corporation or its Shareholders, acts or omissions not in good faith, or self dealing. The Corporation may indemnify the Directors or Officers who are named as defendants in litigation relating to Corporate affairs and the Directors or Officers role therein.

ARTICLE NINE
OFFICERS

The officers of the Corporation will be initially appointed by the Board of Directors. The officers of the Corporation will be at least those required by State law, and any other officers that the Board of Directors may deem necessary. The duties and responsibilities of the Officers will be set by, and will be under the continued direction of, the Directors. Officers may be removed at any time with or without cause, and may resign at any time by delivering written notice to the Board of Directors.

PRESIDENT The President is the principal executive officer of the Corporation and in general supervises and directs the daily business operations of the Corporation, subject to the direction of the Board of Directors. The President is also the proper official to execute contracts, share certificates, and any other document that may be required on behalf of the Corporation. The President shall also preside at all meetings of Directors or meetings of Shareholders.

SECRETARY The Corporate Secretary will in general be responsible for the records of the Corporation which generally includes keeping minutes at any meeting, giving proper notice of any meeting, maintaining the Director and Shareholder registers and transfer records; and along with the President, sign share certificates of the Corporation.

VICE PRESIDENT The Corporate Vice-President if appointed will be responsible for duties to be assigned by the Board of Directors.

TREASURER The Corporate treasurer if appointed will be responsible for duties to be assigned by the Board of Directors.

SECTION 5
BLANK CONSENTS AND MINUTES

INSTRUCTIONS FOR BLANK CONSENTS AND MINUTES

You will remember that the corporation is a separate "person" that cannot physically act for itself, so it acts through its directors. Whenever directors meet to discuss and decide what the corporation will do, the meeting, and what happened, must be recorded. To record your meetings, you may use the enclosed MINUTES OF DIRECTORS MEETING sheets. The recording of meetings and even the meeting itself need not be made over formalized. For example, many people actually formally call the meeting to order; formally ask for turns to speak; formally make, and second motions; and formally adjourn the meeting. This formality comes from directors meetings of large corporations, and is not necessary for small corporate meetings, so don't get caught in this over structured form of meetings. All you need to do is sit down, discuss what needs to be done, vote on the matter, write it all down on one of the minute sheets, and have the secretary sign it. The best way to do this is to write down everything that happens on a plain piece of paper, summarize, and organize the information later, and then record it all on one of the minute sheets.

Even if you have no other meetings, you must have an annual shareholders meeting to "discuss" the results of operations for the year with the shareholders. To simplify this, enclosed is a completed MINUTES OF ANNUAL SHAREHOLDERS MEETING for your use. It contains all the wording required by State law, and all you need to do is sign the appropriate lines and date the form. Many people don't actually hold a meeting, they just sign the minutes of the meeting and file it in the CORPORATE RECORDS binder.

There is another way provided by the bylaws to do all this without having a meeting. It's called taking action by consent, without meeting. You have already used two of them in your incorporating process. The nice thing about consents is that you don't need to actually meet. That comes in handy if you travel a lot. The sheets included in this manual for this are called DIRECTORS CONSENT FOR CORPORATE ACTION WITHOUT MEETING. A consent takes effect when the last person signs it.

All you have to do with a consent is write down what the corporation will do, and have ALL the directors sign, and record their vote on the matter by circling the appropriate letter, Y, N, or A. To be able to use a consent, **all** directors must approve "acting without a meeting" by signing at the bottom of the form. If a director doesn't approve the action being taken, he can vote no by circling N next to his signature, or A, stating that he abstains from voting, but regardless, ALL directors must sign the form.

DIRECTORS CONSENT FOR CORPORATE ACTION WITHOUT MEETING

Pursuant to Virginia Business Corporation Law, the Directors of the Corporation hereby consent to approving actions of the Corporation without a meeting. This consent has the same effect as a meeting vote. By the affirmative vote of a majority of the Directors, as evidenced by the votes and signatures recorded below, the following actions shall be taken:

Copy all forms in this section before using.

(White this out first.)

Director	Y • N • A* Vote	Director	Y • N • A* Vote
Director	Y • N • A* Vote	Director	Y • N • A* Vote
Director	Y • N • A* Vote	Name of Corporation	
Date		SECRETARY	

*As circled by the Director, these abbreviations shall be construed as if they were written out in full, as follows:
Y - Shall be recorded as a yes vote by the director favoring the action.
N - Shall be recorded as a negative vote by the director not favoring the action.
A - Shall be recorded as the Director having declined, or abstained from, voting.

MINUTES OF DIRECTORS MEETING

As required by Virginia Business Corporation Law, the minutes of a meeting of Directors of the Corporation are recorded here. The meeting was held at the offices of the Corporation. Present at the meeting were the Directors who have signed their names below. The signatures below shall constitute waiver by those who have signed of any notice that may be required by law.

Director	Director
Director	Director
Director	Name of Corporation
Date	SECRETARY

MINUTES OF ANNUAL SHAREHOLDERS MEETING

As required by Virginia Business Corporation Law, the minutes of the annual meeting of Shareholders of the Corporation are recorded here. The meeting was held at the offices of the Corporation on the date below. Present at the meeting were the Shareholders who have signed their names below. The signatures below shall constitute waiver of any notice that may be required by law by those who have signed.

After the meeting was duly called to order, it was noted that a quorum of shareholders was present, and the following items of business were conducted:

FIRST The persons who are now Directors were elected to remain Directors until the next annual Shareholders meeting, or until they are removed or resign.

SECOND The persons who are now Officers were elected to remain Officers until the next annual Shareholders meeting, or until they are removed or resign.

THIRD Various items of business were discussed including the financial position of the company, and results of operations for the year just ending. Copies of the income statement and balance sheet shall be attached to these minutes.

FINALLY Having discussed all the items to be discussed at this meeting, it was duly adjourned.

Shareholder	Shareholder
Shareholder	Shareholder
Shareholder	Name of Corporation
Date	SECRETARY

SECTION 6
STARTING AND OPERATING YOUR NEW BUSINESS

STARTING AND OPERATING YOUR NEW BUSINESS

Starting and operating a new business can be a frightening thing, but if you have always worked for someone else and longed to be on your own, it's truly one of the most rewarding experiences you'll ever have in your life. You will be able to see and do things that would never have been possible if you worked for someone else.

But, if you want to keep your business healthy and happy, starting off on the right foot will certainly help. The U.S. Small Business Administration estimates that about 55% of the small businesses that fail each year in this country do not fail because of a lack of knowledge in "their" business or products. They fail because of a lack of general business knowledge. This includes subjects like finance, marketing, and accounting.

While we can't cover all of these subjects in depth, we can share a few principles that you'll need to grasp in order to start a business. Basically there are three areas that you'll have to master in order to succeed in your new business. They are:

1. **Product**
2. **Distribution**
3. **Office**

Product is simply what you sell. Everyone sells something in order to make a living. Although you may actually own and rent apartments for a living, you actually have to sell (rent) them in order to pay your bills. You know more about your product than this book could even begin to tell you, so we will not attempt to do so. However, we will say that in order for your product to survive in todays competitive marketplace, it must:

1. Be a product that people need or want.
People need coats in the winter time. People wanted "pet rocks". Either way, supply a need or a want and you'll do fine.

2. Be competitively priced.
If your product is too expensive, or perceived to be too expensive, sales will never be high enough for you to make a living. Price your product or service in line with your competition, and adjust it from there.

3. Be a quality product.
No one wants to buy a product of poor, or perceived poor quality. If they ever purchase such a product, you can bet that they never will again. Word will spread, and you will soon be out of business.

Distribution is an area that a lot of people overlook. Distribution is simply how you get your product to the customers. This includes everything from advertising to your delivery schedule, both of which are important to Federal Express. You must be able to:

1. Let people know that your product is available, (Advertising)
2. Tell them why they should buy it, (Marketing)
3. Sell it to them, (Sales)
4. Deliver the product to the customer either from your storefront, through the mail, or with your delivery truck. This includes important decisions like, where is the best place to open shop? Should I get a toll free number ? or What is the best time of day to deliver to the west side of town?

As you are beginning to see, distribution is one of the most important areas that you must be skilled in to survive. There are accordingly, volumes written on this subject that are available at your local bookstore, or at the public library.

Office is the title of the tasks that you must master that is closest to the scope of this book, but it is usually the most dreaded of all the tasks outlined above. While product and distribution are subjects that can be learned by combining a little common sense with the knowledge that you have of your product, the "office" heading includes things you may know little or nothing about. For example:

- •OPENING A CHECKING ACCOUNT FOR A CORPORATION
- •OBTAINING A FEDERAL TAX ID NUMBER FOR YOUR BUSINESS
- •STATE TAXES
- •FEDERAL TAXES
- •ACCOUNTING SYSTEMS

Volumes can, and have been written about these subjects. The purpose of this book is to show you step by step how to set up a corporation without a lawyer. But, we feel it our duty to at least briefly explain these subjects in order to help you get started off on the right foot. Mostly, what we want to accomplish in this section is to help familiarize you with some things you may be experiencing for the first time. Remember, if you desire additional information on any of these subjects, visit your local bookstore, library, IRS office, or see your CPA.

OPENING A CHECKING ACCOUNT FOR A CORPORATION

Opening a checking account for a corporation is basically the same as opening one for your sole proprietorship, or yourself personally, except for one thing. The bank will ask you for a corporate resolution. A corporate resolution is simply a document signed by the officers or directors of the corporation stating that you have been given authority to open a checking account for the corporation. Remember that although a corporation can have a checking account, it cannot physically go to the bank and open one. You have to do this for the corporation. The bank simply wants to make sure that the directors of the corporation have given you permission to do so.

Most larger banks will have a blank corporate resolution of their own. The resolution will usually outline things like:

1. The name of the corporation.
2. Who has authority to open accounts on behalf of the corporation.
3. Who has authority to make deposits into corporate accounts.
4. Who has authority to write checks from the corporate accounts.
5. How many signatures are required to sign a check for it to be valid.

In case your bank does not provide one, the form on the next page is a corporate resolution that you can use. The bank officer will need to see you, and all those involved with the corporate checking account sign the form. So if there is more than one person involved with the checkbook, all will need to go to the bank.

CERTIFIED RESOLUTION OF THE BOARD OF DIRECTORS

I, ________________________ do hereby certify that I am the duly elected and qualified Secretary and record keeper of ____ a corporation organized under the laws of the State of _________________________, and that the following is a true ant correct copy of certain resolutions duly adopted at a meeting of the Board of Directors thereof, convened and held in accordance with law, the Charter, the Articles of Incorporation, and bylaws of the corporation. The meeting took place on the ___________day of _____________ 19____. The resolutions are now in force and are included in the records of the corporation.

It is resolved that ____, (hereinafter referred to as the "bank") will be a financial institution of the corporation, and that an account will be opened in the name of, for and on the behalf of the corporation. The name that the accounts will be opened in will be the same as the corporation name shown above.

It is further resolved that delivery to the bank of funds, checks, drafts, or other property, with or without endorsement, will be deposited to the credit of the corporation, and such credits may be withdrawn by check, draft, or other instrument, executed for the corporation by any _______________ of the following individuals.

TITLE	NAME	SIGNATURE
____________	____________________________	________________________
____________	____________________________	________________________
____________	____________________________	________________________
____________	____________________________	________________________
____________	____________________________	________________________

In witness whereof, I affix my signature on this ______ day of___________, 19_____.

____
Secretary

OBTAINING A FEDERAL TAX ID NUMBER FOR YOUR BUSINESS

Basically a Federal tax ID number is a Social Security number for your business. You'll need one if :

1. You have one or more employees (including you and your spouse), or
2. If you have a pension plan, or
3. If you have to pay Federal excise taxes on alcohol, tobacco, or firearm sales.

To get a federal tax ID number, you'll need to get an IRS form, number SS-4 at the IRS office where you live, or by calling the IRS toll-free at **1-800-TAX-1040**. Complete the form and send it to the IRS office that is listed in the instructions for the form. Your number will arrive by mail.

Since the bank will need a tax ID number to open your corporate checking account, you'll probably need your tax ID number faster than the IRS can provide it by mail. **To get your ID number in a hurry**, get a copy of the IRS form SS-4 from the local IRS office or your CPA, complete the form, and then call **1-800-TAX-1040.** When the IRS representative answers, tell him you'd like to get a Federal tax ID number by phone. He will then ask you if you have a completed IRS Form SS-4. Of course, you will answer yes. The representative will either transfer you to someone that will give you the ID number, or give you a special telephone number to call. When you reach the person that assigns the ID numbers, they will basically ask you most of the questions on the form, record the information, and assign you an ID number. You will receive written verification in the mail.

STATE AND LOCAL TAXES

State taxes, of course vary from state to state, and are beyond the scope of this book. But, in order to help you, we have compiled a list of many of the state and local taxes you'll encounter. Usually, when you start your corporation the Corporation Commission will notify many of these taxing authorities for you. If you have any questions about state and local taxes, call the city, the county, and the state dept. of revenue to find out more about them. Their telephone numbers can be found in your telephone directory under the state and local governmental headings.

- •local business tax/permits
- •local general property tax
- •State sales tax
- •State unemployment tax
- •Special sales taxes for beer, gas, mining, etc
- •Hotel/Motel/Entertainment taxes
- •Corporation income/excise tax

FEDERAL TAXES

Other than having to file a corporate income tax return, your most important contact with the Federal government will be withholding taxes. Withholding taxes are what we all have taken out of our hard earned pay every week. Our employer then forwards this money to the government on our behalf. There are three amounts that you will be responsible for paying:

1. Income taxes on employee pay,
2. Social Security (FICA) taxes on employee pay, and
3. FICA matching.

Income taxes and FICA is withheld from employee pay as a percentage of the employee's pay. Basically, when you withhold amounts from your employees pay, you will hold on to the money until the 15th of the next month, at which time you'll deposit the money at your local bank, using a special deposit ticket that the IRS will send you. Plus, at the end of each quarter, you'll file a special withholding tax return with the IRS.

This procedure is simplified by using publications, and attending workshops that the IRS produces at no charge to you. To obtain publications, or find out when workshops will be held, call the IRS toll free at 1-800-TAX-1040. At a minimum, you should obtain these two publications:

1. Publication number 937 entitled "Business Reporting", which explains what is required of you as an employer, and
2. A "Circular E", which explains how, and how much to withhold.

The third type of tax you will become familiar with is what's known as FICA matching. Whenever you withhold FICA (Social Security) taxes from your employee's pay, you will have to pay that same amount to the government for your "FICA matching". Although painful, it's really simple. If you withhold $25 in Social Security taxes from an employee's pay one pay period, you'll have to match that $25, and send the government $50, plus the amount of income taxes you withheld for that employee. All these amounts will be deposited on the 15th of the next month.

ACCOUNTING SYSTEMS

One of the areas that small business people have trouble with the most is accounting. Accounting can be made as simple or as hard as you want it to be. No matter what you do for an accounting system, **do something**. Many people are so afraid of accounting and bookkeeping, that they simply neglect it, and that's when trouble begins.

The most important thing about accounting systems is to simply keep good records of how much money you take in, and how much you spend. If you at least do this, you can pay someone to sort through the records at the end of the year. Your records can be as simple as your checkbook register, or as sophisticated and a computerized bookkeeping system. You will need to keep track of the following items separately:

- Sales
- How much you spent on goods that you resold (cost of goods sold)
- How much you spent on supplies to manufacture your products
- How much you paid employees to manufacture your products
- Compensation of corporate officers
- Salaries and wages of non manufacturing employees
- Repairs of any type
- Amounts that were owed to you and were not paid (if already counted as income)
- Rent
- Taxes - All
- Interest
- Depreciation (amounts expensed periodically for cars, equipment, etc.)
- Depletion (for mining, and oil companies)
- Advertising
- Pension and profit sharing plans
- Employee benefit programs (reimbursement plans, paid vacations, etc.)
- Other deductions

"Other deductions" will include anything not otherwise listed. For these, you will create your own categories, categories like insurance, supplies, and so on. You will need to list these expenses separately on your corporate tax return using your own categories. Also, a piece of advice, the IRS doesn't like the term "MISC. EXPENSES". They want to know exactly what you spent your money on, so don't use the category "MISC" if you can help it.

These categories are from a corporate tax return. If all you do is separate, and keep up with the amount of money you spend on the expenses listed above, all you'll need to do at tax time is write the totals on your corporate income tax return. One of the best books on how to set up and run an accounting system is available from the IRS. Its called "Taxpayers Starting a Business", publication number 583.

We hope this section has been helpful. Thank you for purchasing this book.